THE IRRELEVANT CHURCH

The Irrelevant Church

ROBIN GAMBLE

MONARCH

Eastbourne

Unless otherwise indicated, biblical quotations are from the
New International Version copyright 1973, 1978, 1984
by the International Bible Society.

Front cover painting:
L. S. Lowry, 'Coming from the Mill', 1930.
City of Salford Museums and Art Gallery.

British Library Cataloguing in Publication Data

Gamble, Robin
The irrelevant church
I. Title
261.1

ISBN 1 85424 163 X (Monarch)
0 948704 19 5 (BCGA)

The BCGA acknowledges the financial assistance of the Drummond
Trust, 3 Pitt Terrace, Stirling, in the co-publication of this book.

Printed in Great Britain for
MONARCH PUBLICATIONS LTD
1 St Anne's Road, Eastbourne, E Sussex BN21 3UN by
Richard Clay Ltd, Bungay, Suffolk
Typeset by Nuprint Ltd, Harpenden, Herts.

Contents

Introduction

It has been rather painful writing a book called *The Irrelevant Church*. But then it has been painful, belonging to an irrelevant church over the years. My upbringing on a post-war council estate, my life and work in a succession of struggling urban parishes, my fish-out-of-water experience of theological college and my inner-city ministry today, all speak to me with one voice. Together they shout of the failure of organised Christianity ever to really belong to working-class people. Strange, isn't it, when you think that we have a working-class Saviour?

Most of my life has happened in the city of Bradford; it's a wonderful city, and figures prominently in the pages of this book. Not that this is a book about Bradford. It's a book about cities and towns throughout the country. It's a book about God, and God's church, national, denominational and local. It's a book about how God's church can discard its middle-class, religious corsetry and establish itself as a vital and relevant force in working-class communities.

The Irrelevant Church comes in three sections. They are not designed as three tightly logical pieces of argument flowing consecutively. They are rather three areas of thought, each approaching the one central issue from a slightly different direction. At the end of each section there is a short summary where the issues are sharply re-stated, together with what I hope will be helpful suggestions.

The first section (Chapters 1–3) looks at the church in industrial Britain in the nineteenth century. In so doing, it perhaps explains a little of why things are as they are in the twentieth century. Looking at movements, events and individuals, it shows us errors to avoid repeating, and lessons to put into practice.

The central piece (Chapters 4 and 5) is an examination of biblical teaching about money, greed, equality, social justice and poverty. It discusses these issues on a corporate 'society-wide' scale, and on an individual 'me and mine' scale.

The final three chapters offer a description of the urban situation today, and of what the church nationally and locally should be doing with it. It is my belief that if the church is to be relevant and real for working-class people then it has to do two things. First, it has to speak out against the injustice and unfairness of our national life. Secondly, it has to rediscover the power and direction to become a growing and caring church at the local street level. It has been one of the greatest thrills of my life to be part of a growing, caring inner-city church. While attempting to avoid the blowing of trumpets (in fact ours are more like kazoos than trumpets), I have tried to share a little of the experience that God has led us into.

Some people may be reading this book in order to discover 'the answers', the solution to their difficulties, perhaps hoping to find a neat and tidy list of practical suggestions. If only it were that easy, and where there are one or two paths forward, if only we would follow them. The purpose of this book is not to produce quick solutions, but rather to explore issues. Issues of inequality, justice, church, people and nation. These issues are huge, complex and vital. Many of us have avoided them in the past, or have perhaps approached them with our feelings over-charged and our minds already decided. As we approach these areas afresh we need to read our past in such a way that it will help us to understand our present; to read our Bibles in such a way that they will cast light into the greyness of our heart and mind.

For me, writing this book (and hopefully for you as you read it) there have been three positive results.

First, it has helped me to understand the society in which I live, and forced me to make choices. To choose which side of the fence I will stand on, to choose whose cause I will uphold, to choose what messages I will allow to influence me.

Secondly, it has helped me to understand the church, of which I am a part, and forced me to make changes. To change the way it worships, lives, relates to the community, and communicates its good news.

Thirdly, it has helped me to understand a little bit better the God I try to follow, and forced me to make progress. To make progress in the way I try to love the unloveable, to make progress in the way I try to resist the bad, to make progress in the way I try to be more like Jesus.

I pray that as you read *The Irrelevant Church* you also will find yourself making choices, preparing to make changes and finally making progress. May God be with us all as we try to become a relevant church.

Part I

*The Irrelevant Church
and its History*

CHAPTER ONE

BRITAIN IN THE NINETEENTH CENTURY

British social history of the nineteenth and twentieth centuries is the history of an increasingly urbanised humanity. Men, women and children were sucked into the fast-growing industrial towns and cities, where they were crammed into slum ghettos, which had been quickly erected on the cheap. Many of them had been used to working in their own homes and fields, but they were put to labour in workshops, mines, factories, building sites, shops, rich people's houses, mills and warehouses. In this new world their rural or village styles of relationships, values, religion and superstitions were buried under the struggling and scavenging of city life.

In the good times urban life had much to offer: steady work, companionship, wide ranges of goods, food and drink in the shops, entertainment, bustle and activity. There could be a certain positive boisterousness in the life based around work, home, pubs and chapel. But the good times never lasted quite long enough. Ill health, empty stomachs and blighted hopes always returned sooner or later; usually sooner. In this squalid urban wilderness, the great mass of the inhabitants lived a twilight existence. As new generations of children were born, those that survived childhood came to accept its long labouring days and its lack of hope. They learnt the rules of survival from their parents and adopted their doused-down spirits.

Now, in the second half of the twentieth century, most of the factories and mills have wound down. The fire in the furnaces has been left to go out, while the engine houses have run out of steam. The slums are flattened, replaced by damp, cheaply built council estates. Urban man drives a car, watches a colour telly and goes to Spain for his sand, chips and English beer. Today, however, large-scale urban poverty seems to be making a great come-back (not that it ever really went away). The reins on the enterprise spirit are being loosened, and those lacking strength, education, affluent parents or just good luck, are being left behind as 'also-rans'.

Over the years, there have been a few, but only a few, to listen and to champion the cause of the poor. They have struggled to give families healthy food, modest houses and clean water; to drag children out of the mill and into the classroom, to promise people fresh air to breathe and blue skies to dream about. The political memories, harrowing novels and breathtaking projects of such liberal-minded English men and women are with us today, to excite and inspire. In the end, however, the real struggle, the struggle for fair wages and political equality, for space to live and a future to move into, was achieved by the working people, working together. How real their achievements are for today's urban poor still remains to be seen.

Throughout this period, the church generally has managed to keep its distance. It has mixed with the right sort of people, taking their sons to be its clergy, sharing in their politics and adapting their systems of respectable morality. It has maintained a sense of good taste around its worship, architecture and theology, while having the odd moment of exciting cautious thinking which has occasionally led to cautious, cautious action.

There have been outbreaks of enthusiasm and even of revival among the poor, but the institution has always managed to regain control before things got completely out of hand. The church has not ignored the poor; it has erected buildings for them, visited them and regularly ladled out charity to them.

There have of course been exceptions: exceptional men and women with compassion, power and ability, who have stood out and spoken out; exceptional movements and events, when the flame has burnt brightly. For all of these we thank God, and ask what can we learn from the blaze of their lives and missions.

The Industrial Revolution

The Industrial Revolution began in the latter stages of the eighteenth century and ran through to the middle decades of the nineteenth. In one sense it was neither purely industrial (for there were changes in agriculture and commerce that were all part of the same process), nor was it revolutionary (for the changes took place over an extended period of time rather than a short period). Nevertheless, the term still sticks, and sparks off pictures in our imagination of smoking chimneys, blazing furnaces and clanking mills. In essence it consisted of the following factors:

> Technological improvements, especially in the iron, steel and textile industries; the introduction and development of steam power.

> Huge improvements in the transport system, first in roads and canals, and later in the building of the railways.

> Developments in commerce resulting in bigger banks, less liable to collapse and able to offer greater stability. The flow of money was also increased, making capital easier to obtain.

> A massive growth in the national population, and a colossal concentration of population in the mining and manufacturing areas.

The main areas of activity were South Wales, the West Midlands, Lancashire, the West Riding of Yorkshire and the North East. In these areas raw materials, power and population were brought together in a way that the world had never seen before.

The results were at once gloriously uplifting and witheringly degrading. For a few it meant fabulous wealth, but for many it meant the crushing of hope and the ending of dignity.

The Industrial Revolution created a physical landscape and a spiritual landscape which are still with us. The church, comprising all denominations, is called to occupy, to live within, to be incarnated into this landscape. Once there, it is the task of the church to be effective in evangelism and to discover meaningful patterns of spirituality, worship and communication. Leaders, disciples and gifted men and women need to be raised up and equipped from within. This is the response that God was looking for during the nineteenth century; it is the response he is still looking for.

'Whilst the engine runs, the people must work'

In 1811, a third of the British workforce was employed in agriculture. By 1851 this figure had fallen to a tenth. Thus, Britain's workforce was urbanised and to a large extent industrialised, although surprisingly, by as late as 1851, still only 25% worked in large factories or mines. Most still worked in small workshops (eg the nailworkers of the West Midlands and many of the weavers of the West Riding) or sweatshops (eg the tailors of the East End of London). The service industry, domestic service, building and construction were all large-scale employers.

For the industrial workforce, their labour was virtual slavery. The working day was long (twelve to thirteen hours in the mills, usually longer in the workshops) while life was short (forty years was not unusual). There was a constant risk of injuries, especially in textiles and mining, and an unhealthy working environment. Women and girls working in the match factories of East London lost teeth and often their lower jaw through sulphur poisoning; those employed in the potteries suffered rheumatism due to the damp; while the miners were often broken prematurely by cancer and ruptures. Women (even at the height of their pregnancies) and small children were pressed into labour alongside the men, and forced to sweat in the extremes of heat and cold, of dampness and darkness. A woman of thirty-seven described her work thus:

> I have a belt round my waist, and a chain passing between my legs, and I go on my hands and feet. The road is very steep and we have to hold by a rope, and when there is no rope, by anything we can catch hold of.... The pit is very wet where I work, and the water comes over our clog tops always, and I have seen it up to my thighs; it rains in at the roof terribly; my clothes are wet through almost all day long.... I have drawn till I have the skin off me; the belt and chain is worse when we are in the family way. My feller (husband) has beat me many a time for not being ready.[1]

'The walls are only half-a-brick thick'

The industrial areas became boom areas as people flocked to them to find work. The national population doubled from 10.5 million to 21 million between 1801 and 1851, but most of the boom towns saw a much bigger rate of increase. Bradford's population had actually been falling before the Industrial Revolution, but this quickly changed as the town became known as 'Worstedopolis'. From 1801 to 1851 Bradford's population rose from 13,264 to 103,778—an eightfold increase, greater than any other town or city in the country. Bradford's displaced thousands came from all over the country but especially from Lancashire, East Anglia and the West Country. There was also a sizeable minority group of Irish immigrants, around 8,600 in 1851.

These teeming thousands of the new industrial cities were housed in quickly thrown-up slum dwellings. Tiny back-to-back houses squeezed around foul-smelling courtyards, with an average of five or six persons per room in Bradford in 1845. Sometimes up to twenty families shared one earthen privy, so there was no chance of anything remotely approaching hygienic conditions. In these rat-holes they lived, slept, sometimes worked, even kept some animals, and almost always died too soon. The

average age of death in Bradford was eighteen years, compared to
thirty-four for Kendal. While the gentry and professional classes
of the town enjoyed a life-expectancy of thirty-eight years, the
woolcombers could look forward to a meagre sixteen. Bradford
had no proper drainage either above or below ground until the
1860s; fresh water was purchased from a cart, three gallons for a
penny. Here privacy, freedom, space and quiet were unthinkable;
large families of shrieking, hungry children, open filth and squalor, and occasional cholera epidemics were the order of the day.[2]

> A hoard of ragged women and children swarm about, as filthy as the
> swine that thrive upon the garbage heaps and in the puddles.... The
> race that lives in these ruinous cottages behind broken windows
> mended with oilskin, sprung doors and rotten door-posts, or in dark
> wet cellars in measureless filth and stench... must really have reached
> the lowest stage of humanity.... In each of these pens, containing at
> most two rooms, a garret and perhaps a cellar, on the average, twenty
> human beings live.... For each 120 persons, one usually inaccessible
> privy is provided...

> How beautiful is the smoke,
> The smoke of Bradford
> Pouring from numberless chimney stacks,
> Condensing and falling in showers of blacks
> All around and upon the ground,
> In house and street and yard,
> Or adding grace to the thoughtless face
> Of yourself or the man you meet,
> Now in the eye, now in the nose,
> How beautiful is the smoke.[3]

Wages in most industries (including agriculture) were almost
always poor, and shrank to below subsistence level in poor times.
In Bradford this led to the famous woolcombers' strike of 1825, a
time when the City Fathers, now remembered so fondly, showed
their true hardness and lack of compassion. However, wages for
most industrial workers rose in the second half of the century,

enabling a richer lifestyle of varied diets, some consumer goods and new leisure opportunities. Harsh fines were usually imposed for poor time-keeping and similar offences, and there was no security of contract, compensation, sick pay, etc. Bradford's main sources of employment were iron and coal mines, iron works and worsted textiles. Of these, textiles was the biggest employer, and the pay and conditions were particularly bad. The weavers of the West Riding had traditionally enjoyed a relatively prosperous lifestyle, working at home or in small workshops, often operating as a tight family work unit and perhaps maintaining a small parcel of land. Industrialisation saw a large drop in their earnings, and with mechanisation of the weaving process in the 1860s, they were pushed into huge, impersonal, clanging mills. Employment was often given only to their women and children who then had to support their men.

This working and living environment was built by a relatively small group of speculators and mill owners, the men who had made and were continuing to make huge fortunes out of Britain's industrial hegemony. These were the sort of men who firmly believed that what was good for Bradford businessmen, was good for Bradford. The huge scale of their affluence is well conserved today in the Gothic civic buildings they 'gave' to the people, in the rows of fine Victorian villas they built, and in the crudely ostentatious tombs of these City Fathers.

Laissez-faire and revolution

The political climate which allowed this exploitation of human labour and the creation of inhumane human dwellings had two main lines of thought.

The first was the economic doctrine of *laissez-faire*, leaving things to look after themselves, giving commerce and industry the freedom to develop, allowing the captains of industry the elbow-room to make their profits. The government saw no need to interfere, or to improve regulations on work and health conditions; they left the market to regulate and run itself. Behind this 'hands-off' approach was the economic thinking of Adam Smith, that prosperity for all social classes would best be achieved by an unfettered open market. The upper-class fear, that the population of the lower classes would explode if they were too well fed and cared for, also fuelled this belief. The combined effect meant that there was no one to protect the weak, the poor and the vulnerable from the rampant excesses of capitalism. *Laissez-faire* was a very real barrier that had to be slowly overcome by the great social reforms of the first half of the century.

The second line of thought was that of revolution. The French Revolution of 1789 had at first been welcomed in this country by the middle classes. This warm welcome turned to massive fear and rejection as the full story of the horrors emerged. The upper and middle classes of England began seeing revolution everywhere, and were determined to use all force to stamp it out. Despite these huge fears, and the vicious attacks on working-class people that they produced, it is very doubtful whether at any stage in the century this country was ever in imminent danger of violent revolution. Nevertheless, the working classes were affected by these distant rumblings and their own aspirations for decent wages and living conditions and political equality were encouraged and excited.

Divided political allegiance

The Anglican world of Trollope's *Barchester Towers* stood four-square with the establishment of crown, aristocracy and Toryism. It buttressed *laissez-faire* and the class-divided structures of society. It shared the Establishment's over-reaction to any form of insurgence. Charlotte Bronte's novel *Shirley* gives a good example of an Anglican minister in the West Riding of the late eighteenth century, who literally takes up arms against the machine-breakers, never thinking to enquire into their grievances or problems.

In contrast, the Nonconformists and Roman Catholics were generally Liberal/Whig/Radical and middle class, despite the fact that the Wesleys themselves had been high Tories. They were committed to the struggle for political reform and the extending of franchise.

The political and religious leaders of both sides, however, were united in their rejection of working-class claims to be considered and empowered politically. Working-class leaders had worked with the nonconformist Liberal groups in the campaign for reform. When the Great Reform Act came in 1832 it gave the vote to many middle-class and some higher working-class males, but the vast bulk of the lower classes was left out in the political cold, and there they were left to struggle on alone, first through the Chartist movement and then through the efforts of the unions. The political situation is captured in *Felix Holt*, a novel by George Eliot. The novel depicts the landed aristocrats of the industrial Midlands allied to Anglicanism, in the form of the local parish church. The political opposition comes from the Radical candidate supported by the local nonconformist and free-thinking working-class man, who has not even got the vote. The painful irony of the book is that neither side really appreciated or cared for the working-class people; they were below the level of interest.

Felix Holt is one of the great working-class heroes of nineteenth-century literature. Another is Thomas Hardy's Jude, in *Jude the Obscure*. Jude is a self-educated working man feeling a vocation to the ministry. However, his lowly background, his social class and lack of academic standards mean he is not good enough for the church. Both writers were making profound observations on the society, the false standards and most shocking of all, on the Christian church of their day.

These then were the working, living, political and spiritual conditions of life for the majority of people in the nineteenth century. In every age the church is called to be a community of love, and to have a message of good news, freedom for the

CHAPTER TWO

THE CHURCHES AND THE WORKING CLASSES

The early nineteenth century

At the beginning of the nineteenth century, the majority of the population of England, irrespective of class or region, probably considered themselves to belong to the Church of England. In this one sense at least the Church of England was the church of the people. However, behind this healthy facade there were two major areas of ill-health. The first concerned the degree of understanding and commitment behind those millions of loose affiliations, and the second concerned the actual state of the Church of England.

In the early nineteenth century most people still lived in a rural setting, on the land itself or in a village or small country town. This picture would change very soon with the mushrooming of the industrial towns. Traditionally the picture of these country dwellers turning up to church week by week, with full stomachs and thankful hearts, has been contrasted with that of the urban poor, wretched and godless. Thus the argument goes that the Christian poor of England lost their Christianity when they emigrated to the smoke.

In fact this picture of happy and healthy rural England is a myth. The agricultural world of the novels of Thomas Hardy

27

(one of the most clear-sighted observers of the English countryside) is peopled by a varied rag-bag of wretched farm labourers and their dependants. These characters are usually struggling to hang on to their dwellings; eating a very plain diet most of the time; and holding on to a strange collection of beliefs consisting of superstition, country folklore, and affiliation to religious indifference.

James Obelkevich has carried out a meticulous study of South Lindsey (an area of North Lincolnshire) and of its religious habits between 1825 and 1875.[1] He demonstrated a very real class structure in rural religion: the upper classes were generally Anglican, very private in their beliefs. The independent farmers and village traders were mostly Methodists, stressing the need for self-improvement. The poor labourers had very little personal belief and commitment. They went to the local vicar and the church for charity, and to the local chapel for a strong social life and Saturday night entertainment.

In parishes where the local landowner was resident and went to church, a large percentage of his labouring workforce went too, but when he stayed away, they also stayed away. The actual beliefs of the poorer classes contained a good deal of superstition and virtual pagan nature religion. As the century wore on, membership declined, the political awareness of the labouring men took them even further from Christianity, and women came to dominate congregations. As church and chapel became aware of their failures to attract adults after 1860, they both concentrated on children's work. The Primitive Methodists, who had had a very sharp edge to their gospel preaching, came to concentrate more on social life and weekend entertainments.

The Church of England

Despite the strong evangelical movement within the Church of England in the late eighteenth century, the church was still in a decayed state. In many parishes the priest was absent for long periods of time. One reason for this was the practice of one priest holding various parishes; this had financial advantages for the individual priest but spiritual disadvantages for the parishes. The whole system of who was appointed to which parish was corrupt (though the Bishops did attempt to change the multiple benefice system in the early part of the nineteenth century). In many areas the parish priest formed an unholy alliance with the local squire or landowner. The church's life of worship, prayer and mission was often dead or dying, its clergy were untrained and its buildings were inadequate and in the wrong places.

If the church was a failure in the countryside, among the rural poor, it was an open disaster in the booming towns among the industrial poor, although it must be remembered that we are talking in generalisations and there were of course exceptions.

The Nonconformist churches

The first half of the nineteenth century was a time of explosive growth for the Nonconformists. They were developing work in the industrial areas years before Anglicanism woke up to the new facts of life. For example, Dukinfield in Lancashire had built up a population of 10,000 before an Anglican church was built in 1848, by which time there were seventeen chapels in the town. In the West Riding licenses issued for new nonconformist places of worship increased from seventy-three in the 1780s to 401 in the 1790s. In this period the Methodists saw their membership increase ninefold, the Independent Congregationalists increased sixfold, whilst the Baptists saw a sevenfold increase. This huge increase is still not completely understood, but it seems to have been caused by various factors.

Part of it seems to have been to do with class-consciousness, but there are two rival theories as to how this operated. E. P. Thomson, a left-wing historian, argues that when the political radical movement of the late eighteenth century was squashed, the working-class men were in despair and turned to Methodism for compensation.[2] Hobsbawm, a Marxist historian, and Gilbert, a church social historian, argue that the Methodist success among the working class was not in reaction to political failure but was actually part of the same process of growing class awareness and solidarity.[3]

Many of the men involved as Luddites, or in revolutionary political groups in the West Riding at the beginning of the nineteenth century, were also strong Methodists, their political and religious passions seeming to feed each other. Later on, Chartism, the first working-class mass political movement, was certainly very strong in the big cities. Bradford, for example, witnessed riots, huge marches to close down local mills and even an attempted uprising, during the 1830s and 1840s. At the same time nonconformist Christianity was also a powerful driving force in the life of the town. The two movements seem to have run side by side, and may well have served to nurture and give momentum to each other during this period.

For the thousands of displaced persons flocking into new towns, the local chapel may have been the only point of stability in their life. Often it established itself as the focus for community life, especially in the smaller towns and villages. Local employers and industrialists often encouraged and used chapel religion as a means of producing a well-disciplined, hard-working and non-revolutionary workforce: pressure was put on workers to be seen to be regular Sunday attenders.

Apart from these sociological factors there was also the spiritual dynamic. In a grey, hostile and hopeless world, people were attracted to the gospel. Furthermore, where the gospel was preached in an unashamedly open and impassioned way, it broke right through to the very lowest elements of society.

In Bradford, the 1851 census figures of Horace Mann show that 14,000 Bradfordians were at a place of public Christian worship on a typical Sunday. (This means that Bradford, along with Manchester, had the lowest percentage of church attendance of any city in the country.) Of these only 16% were Anglicans while the city's large immigrant Irish population accounted for 22% being Roman Catholic. The remaining 62% were chapel-goers, of whom most were probably middle class and higher working class. The census also reveals that all the Bradford churches and chapels combined could only be expected to provide enough seats for a third of the possible church-attending population.

The churches' failure among the urban poor

Most of the nonconformist membership growth was amongst the middle and higher working classes. Professionals, tradesmen and skilled artisans were generally well represented in the church pews, but the unskilled masses from mine, mill and building site etc were absent.

These were people who had never had a strong belief when they had lived in the countryside. When they settled in the towns they automatically identified the local Anglicans and Nonconformists as being culturally and politically alien. In an age when politics were very important to people, political differences represented big social divisions. Very often the pub was their church and cheap beer, spirits and tobacco their religious experience. In this pub world they found a solace, a warmth of friendship and acceptance that they never found at church or chapel.

They may have actually been pushed into part of a large town where there was no local church to belong to, even if they wanted to. If they did decide to go along to a place of worship they would have been asked to pay for the privilege of sitting in a pew, while the fine clothes and mannerisms of their fellow-worshippers would have aggravated their sense of inferiority. Many of these poorer masses were illiterate, and what religious experience they had had in the past had often contained a strong emotional, semi-magical element. In contrast, Protestant worship of church and chapel was book-orientated, often very intellectual with its heavy dependence on reading, listening and thinking logically. Moreover, the minister leading the service and preaching the sermon was usually from a distant social and educational background.

Nevertheless, there were exceptions to these general patterns. The Nailers of the West Midlands were unskilled lower-working-class industrial workers, yet they were strong and believing members of their chapels, and there were also the Ranters.

The Ranters

The denomination which got closest to the working classes in the nineteenth century was the Primitive Methodists or Ranters. After the death of the Wesley brothers the mainstream Methodist Church moved away from its humble origins and methods. Under the autocratic, right-wing leadership of Jabez Bunting, power and leadership were centralised, huge ostentatious chapels were built, the minister became a professional and trained man, and the Methodist Church quite consciously moved 'up-market'.

The Primitive Methodists were a breakaway group who wanted to get back to the simple, evangelising roots of the first Methodists. They were formed in 1811 in the Cheshire and Staffordshire region after their two leaders Hugh Bourne and William Clowes were expelled by the Methodist Conference; both had been involved in evangelism for some years before this decision. In 1807 Bourne had introduced the idea of the 'camp meeting', ie evangelism under canvas, from America. It proved to be successful but was condemned by the Methodist Conference as 'highly improper'. (The expulsion of Bourne and Clowes from a formalised denomination and their subsequent establishing of a very alive one bears a remarkable similarity to the case of the Wesleys themselves.)

The Primitive Methodists had a simple fundamentalist theology of heaven and hell, of sin, repentance and conversion. Their preachers were 'ranters', powerful, impassioned, often poorly educated, but strong in faith and expectancy. They were able to speak to working people in their own language and style. Their services were alive, exciting, often emotional and very experience-orientated. Women were prominent in the movement: Elizabeth Russell was one of their leading evangelists in Wiltshire and

Berkshire in the 1820s and 1830s (this was another reason for the Ranters' rejection by Calvinistic Methodists and Anglicanism). They were often deeply involved in working-class politics. Joseph Arch, the founder of the National Agricultural Labourers' Union, was a Primitive Methodist, as were most of its other leading lights. Arch, who set up the Union to fight against rural poverty in the 1870s, was known to his followers as 'our man, our Joe, the labourers' hope, apostle, friend.' Similarly the coal strikes of the 1830s and 1840s in the North East depended very much on the leadership of the Ranter preachers.

The Ranters gave to many poor people, in town and countryside, a genuine conversion and experience of God for the first time in their lives. They gave them a new human dignity, taught them new standards of family life and personal morality and self-discipline. At their height they numbered about 200,000, a powerful and exciting group of Christians. We can learn much from the faith, enthusiasm, and local working-class leadership which led to their rise. Sadly we also have to learn from the conflict of movement and institution which was to lead to their decline in later years.

The later nineteenth century

During the second half of the nineteenth century, the churches' failure to reach the urban masses became a major discussion point in all denominations. The Church of England in particular made a huge effort at internal reform and external growth in the cities. For the Nonconformists, however, the gap between chapel and working class continued to widen. The Roman Catholics experienced continuous growth due principally to immigration, and the Salvation Army burst onto the scene with evangelistic zeal and joy.

Anglican reform and resurgence

The period of 1740–1830 had been one of overall decline for the Church of England. It had failed to anticipate and respond to the new industrial cities. However it at last began to wake up during the middle decades of the century. Its failure to penetrate the large cities and reach the 'working man' was suddenly on every agenda from National Convocation down to parish sermons. The question was addressed by such leading churchmen as the Dean of Westminster (who wanted to open the Abbey up to working people) and William Thomson, the Archbishop of York. The Bishop of Peterborough, William Magee, described it as the 'one great issue of our time, before which all others fade into insignificance.'

This great debate produced real action. There was a wave of church building and improvement, producing over 4,000 new churches in poorer areas. This was provided for by the Ecclesiastical Commissioners shifting resources, by obtaining various loans from the State and by the setting up of numerous funds and societies often at diocesan level. The building of new churches went hand in hand with other institutional reforms and the setting up of new urban dioceses such as Manchester and Liverpool.

The combined effects of the Evangelical Revival, the Oxford Movement and the influence of the Christian Socialists was to produce a broadly based spiritual renewal, affecting 'Low', 'High' and 'Middle' Church. Standards of worship, prayer, faith, vocation and clergy training were all improved. A new quality of clergy, often full of zeal and ability, began to feel a missionary pull to the big cities in the second half of the century, although the response from Evangelicals was probably less than from others. However, being an Anglican clergyman remained very much the prerogative of gentlemen. Most of the industrial parishes were not able to offer a decent wage, so the clergy needed private means. There was certainly no opportunity for local working-class men to get anywhere near the Anglican priesthood.

Evangelism was suddenly, and massively, on the Church of England's agenda. Missionary priests and brotherhoods, mission churches and colleges all sprang up, often in large numbers. A college to train lay evangelists in East London was established by the SPCK. The idea of evangelistic parish missions was popularised in the 1880s by George Body. Many societies and organisations were set up to stimulate evangelism in industrial areas, including the Church Pastoral Aid Society in 1836 and The Church of England Working Men's Society in 1876. In 1882 William Carlile formed the Church Army as an evangelistic wing to the Church of England's work. By the turn of the century the Church Army had over 600 nurses and evangelists in parishes and sixty-five mobile 'vans' on the road.

All of this combined thought and activity represents perhaps the one occasion in the history of Anglicanism when the Church of England has adopted an evangelistic growth mode as opposed to its traditional pastoral and maintenance mode. Interestingly, this period of 1830–1914 remains as the only extensive period between the Reformation and the present day to see a reverse in its general membership decline. Numbers of Easter communicants rose from approximately 605,000 in 1830 to 2,260,000 in 1914.

Methodists and the independents

There is no accepted fixed pattern about working-class membership of the churches in the second half of the nineteenth century. Gilbert's careful analysis of statistics leads him to the conclusion that Nonconformist growth came to a halt around 1840 and that thereafter attention was concentrated more on the middle classes. In contrast, Bishop Ted Wickham's localised studies of church and chapel building in Sheffield[4] points to a continued growth among the working classes but with the Church of England leading the way. Similar studies in Oldham by Joyce[5] also show continued local growth. The historian Inglis argues persuasively that Nonconformity never really succeeded in the big cities. He sees Methodism as a predominantly lower-middle-class religion strong in the villages and small towns, while the independents (Baptists and Congregationalists) catered for the liberal middle-class industrialists.[6]

In 1851 Horace Mann organised a national census to see just how many people were present at public Christian worship on a typical Sunday. Mann's figures of approximately 40% of the population should probably be scaled down slightly, due to double attendence. Today we would consider such a result to be miraculously high, but to the Victorians, they were a disappointment. Commenting on them, Mann referred to the growing secularisation (ie the process whereby religious beliefs and practices are replaced by non-religious ones) in society. He and many others were particularly shocked that 'the masses of our working population are never or but seldom seen in our religious congregations.' The feelings of many concerned commentators are well summed up by Engels' remarks:

> All bourgeois writers are agreed that the workers, have no religion and do not go to church. Exceptions to this are the Irish, a few older workers and those wage-earners who have one foot in the middle class, camp-overlookers, foremen and so on. Among the mass of the working-class population, however, one nearly always finds an utter indifference to religion.... The mere cry 'He's a parson' is often enough to force a clergyman off the platform (Hopkins, p 81).

As we have already seen, the churches generally (though with a few exceptions) had never really converted and discipled either the rural poor or the new industrial poor. A tradition had been established, and strongly reinforced by time, that the working classes did not go to church. This situation seemed to get worse rather than better in the second half of the century, as various factors combined to make both church and chapel part of the middle-class and higher working-class environment.

For instance, many Nonconformists made a conscious bid for the middle classes. In what one Wesleyan historian called 'our

Mahogany Period' they built fine distinguished chapels. These were financed by putting up pew rents, not only of the best pews but also of those normally reserved for the poor. Thus the lower classes were literally priced out of the market.

Class divisions seem to have had a growing influence. In one Glasgow chapel the wealthy morning congregation complained that the poor people who came at night were a health risk to them. The industrial poor were made increasingly aware that their clothing, their smell, their language, their habits—in fact their poverty—were out of place in the grand religious establishments of the later nineteenth century.

At the same time, Nonconformists tended to move away from preaching the 'simple gospel'. They replaced it by teaching middle-class respectability, teetotalism, self-help and prosperity. One missioner in Aberdeen is actually recorded as seriously doubting the reality of many of the poor people's conversion, simply because they were not prospering financially. Thus the sharp evangelistic edge of many churches and chapels was blunted. Moreover, when what has been termed 'the fading of Puritanism' gathered momentum in the latter decades of the century, it was the Nonconformists who were hardest hit.

Further challenges to and weakening of the Christian message came from another source. The nineteenth century saw a huge growth in intellectual atheism, agnosticism and doubt. The church's poor handling of the Darwinian debate and the emergence of liberal critical theology both served to weaken the intellectual fibre of the church.

Sociological changes in the make-up of society also often had a negative impact on the churches. Big businesses began to replace smaller ones, and at the same time reduced the employer's pressure on his workforce to be in chapel on Sunday. The gradual movement of the higher middle classes out to the suburbs took leadership and finance away from the oldest chapels. As the State gradually assumed responsibility for education and for providing some welfare services, the churches partially lost a role. Finally, throughout the second half of the century wages generally were rising, and the working classes were becoming more prosperous and widening their leisure pursuits: gardening, railway excursions, music-halls and football all challenged their church-going.

In the late nineteenth and early twentieth centuries the emergence of 'mass unions' and the Labour movement challenged the loyalty of many working-class Christian people. There were attempts to hold the two together by setting up Chartist Churches and later Labour Churches. Many of the new Labour leaders were actually products of the chapels and of the teetotal movements. Keir Hardie had a conversion experience and signed the pledge at the age of twenty-two. His Christianity had a strong influence on his political views, but he became increasingly frustrated with bad employers and with the affluence and hypocrisy he saw in the church, and moved in a left-wing direction.

In South Wales the leaders of the chapels were generally liberals, while the mass membership were usually Independent Labour Party (ILP). In North Wales, the quarry strike at Bethesda, 1900–1903, set Anglican quarry owners against a Methodist workforce buttressed by the local chapels. The strike was broken by Anglicans actually continuing to work. These sorts of divisions forced many men who were concerned for their political and economic freedom to leave church and chapel.

The huge gulf that thus opened up between the churches and the working classes is nowhere better illustrated than in Robert Tressell's novel *The Ragged-Trousered Philanthropists*. The hero of the novel is a working man called Owen. He is a thinking socialist, a genuinely good man who desires social justice, decent food for his wife and a future for his children. At every point, however, Owen is confronted by employers, local politicians, ministers of religion, Sunday school superintendents, etc, all of whom form a united group. They are all better fed, dressed and housed than him, his family and his workmates, and are oblivious of the poverty that surrounds them. Their religion is seen as empty and hypocritical.

The home mission front

Nonconformity did make some attempt to reach the lower classes in the big cities, but it was always a fairly limited attempt and it met with very limited success. Most of the denominations set up some sort of home missionary activities. Resources however were usually very small and were often committed more to rural than to urban situations.

The Pleasant Sunday Afternoon movement was set up by John Blackham in 1875 and had some success, especially in the Midlands. It set out to create non-denominational 'easy to enter into' religious meetings on Sunday afternoons. The main denominations, however, were never really happy with the idea and it faded in the early twentieth century.

There was a handful of exceptional preachers who managed to build up huge personal followings in urban areas. They often used public halls to reach the non-churchgoing public, and employed large-scale advertising. Charles Leach in Birmingham and Spurgeon in London were among the most famous, and they were followed by the popularist evangelistic campaigns of Moody and Sankey in 1875.

In 1885 the Methodists established the London Wesleyan Mission to bring evangelism to the heart of the city. The project had some success, and by 1909 over forty towns and cities had their own central missions, separate from their traditional circuit structures. This should probably be seen as the Methodists' biggest single development in urban mission during the whole century. It had certainly produced some sort of local fruit, but it could only ever hope to touch a very few of the masses, and certainly never represented a major shift in practice.

The Primitive Methodists

Developments within Primitive Methodism contain various of these wider movements. In the middle decades of the nineteenth century, they began to move away from their earlier Ranter image. Wanting to consolidate, they built big chapels and set up a central bureaucracy. Much of the movement came under the control of rich individuals such as Sir William Hartley (the jam maker) who built a theological college and introduced academic training for an increasingly professional ministry. They seemed to have gradually become 'more at home in this world', leaving their emotionalism and evangelism behind, and replacing their radical working-class politics with a more liberal approach. Their adoption of teetotalism and Victorian respectability virtually amounted to a replacement of 'salvation by grace' by 'salvation by works'; 'signing the pledge' often became more important than individual conversion.

However, the pattern in the later nineteenth century is not exclusively one of general decline; the Salvation Army came into existence as a very fiery grouping, and the Roman Catholics were established as a major religious power among the poor.

The Salvation Army

The Salvation Army was founded by General and Mrs Booth in 1877. It developed out of their evangelistic tent missions first set up in Whitechapel in 1875. Like others before them, their use of populist and revivalist methods in a formalised and stiff denomination (in this case the Methodists) was frowned upon and they had to leave.

The army of Salvationists which they established had a particular concern for the poor and needy. Its message emphasised the simple gospel and the need for conversion. It was passionately opposed to all 'worldly pleasures', especially drink. Booth established a religious group to fill the gap between the conventional churches and the masses. He structured it on military lines around his own autocratic leadership, and placed women in a very prominent position. The Army in effect took the place of the Wesleys and the Ranters in the late nineteenth century. Their Holiness Gatherings, witnessing the outpouring of the Holy Spirit, their enthusiastic fervour and joy in the face of often violent opposition and their fiery working-class preachers made them a vital spiritual force in their heyday of the 1880s. K. S. Inglis describes them as 'the only Christian evangelists of their time who approached working-class non-worshippers at their own cultural level.' At their height they had a membership of over 100,000 and were selling over 300,000 copies of the *War Cry* per week.

In 1890 General Booth published his great work *In Darkest England and the Way Out*. This represented a major shift in his thinking and in the strategy of the Army. In the past drink had been seen as the enemy, and the creator of poverty: now Booth was looking beyond this at people's unemployment, housing squalor and complete social deprivation. The Army opened up a whole new area of work, concentrating on social and community improvement.

By the early twentieth century, there were signs of the inevitable institutionalism robbing the army of its simple enthusiasm. The fire had not exactly gone out, but it was certainly well under control in a strong fireplace. The biography of Smith Wigglesworth, the Bradford-born healer and evangelist, describes how his wife, herself a gifted evangelist, became disillusioned with the Army and felt the need to leave it.[7]

The Roman Catholics

The Roman Catholic Church was in a state of steady decline in this country until late in the eighteenth century. It was then that large-scale building projects began bringing over Irish navvies, who subsequently began to register their religious affiliations. This movement was intensified in the 1830s and 1840s with the huge labour demands of the new industries and with the pressure of the Irish potato famine. Irish ghettos were soon established, not by the immigrants themselves, but by the dynamics of the housing market. Thus in a town like Bradford the Irish were paid the worst wages and were pushed into the very worst and most overcrowded parts of the city, eg the Broomfields and Bedford Square area, Westgate and Wapping. The Irish presence was particularly strong in the North West of England and Western

Scotland. There were sectarian riots in Liverpool in 1891 which then spread to Glasgow and Preston. It seems that in some areas this religious sectarianism was actually exploited by some Tory politicians and clergy as a means of establishing a power base among the Protestant working classes.

In 1780 there was an estimated Roman Catholic membership of 70,000. By 1851 this had grown to 900,000 and by 1913 to 1,800,000, although this probably represents only about 960,000 actually attending Mass. These figures contain the rump of old English Catholic families and a steady, though relatively small, stream of converts from middle-class intellectualism. In the main, however, they represent a large slice of the industrial working classes.

During the twentieth century the Roman Catholic Church has managed to hold on to its working-class membership more effectively than any other denomination. (Since the 1960s, however, attendances at weekly Mass have declined sharply.) Part of the reason for this is the cultural one, that the Irish were able to hold on to their Irishness best when their communities were centred around the strongest single link with their roots, which was their religion. There was also, however, a thorough use of symbolism and ritual which are particularly helpful to a non-book-orientated class of people. The ritualistic traditions of Catholicism probably speak much stronger to working-class people than do the 'bookish' traditions of Protestantism. Furthermore, the Catholics continued to recruit and import their priests from the same working-class Irish roots whence had come their congregations. Irish Roman Catholic and working-class Christians were able to identify with their spiritual leaders much more than their Protestant working-class neighbours were able to identify with Protestant clergy.

The compassionate few

As huge institutions, the churches tried to respond to industrialisation. They organised and sometimes reorganised, they hoped for growth and eventually experienced decline. Ultimately they failed to understand, to communicate with and to care for the working classes. Alongside these huge institutional developments was the work of a handful of individuals and small groups. These individuals were reformers, pushing their noses into the conditions of factories and prisons; they were writers, trying to tell the one half of Victorian Britain what life was like for the other; they were evangelists, healers and carers, trying to go where Jesus had gone before. They were not all Christians, although an amazingly high number of them were. Most of them worked in small obscure corners of the grey cities and have now been largely forgotten. Some of them, however, occupied centre stage and had a huge influence in their day. Their work still holds wisdom and power for our day.

The Clapham Sect

This was a group of wealthy, politically influential, evangelical Christians, operating in the early years of the nineteenth century. They were concerned for mankind's social and spiritual welfare, but they seem to have had no interest in his political need for equality. They were not democrats but paternalists, looking down on the poor and needy from their own lofty position of privilege. Nevertheless they did a great deal of good for the needy, and prepared the way for others. They were a very tightly based spiritual group led by William Wilberforce. His and their greatest victory was the ending of the slave trade, although they were involved in many other movements both home and abroad, including factory reform. Throughout their compaigning they used their personal wealth and political influence, and were motivated by their evangelical zeal.

Elizabeth Fry

Elizabeth Fry was probably the best known representative of the Quaker tradition of social involvement. Of all Christian groups the Society of Friends has probably been the most consistent in its beliefs of human equality, the need for social reform, and peace and justice. Thus when early industrialists visited the Quaker iron-making entrepreneurs of Coalbroakdale, at the beginning of the Industrial Revolution, they remarked on how these enormously rich men ate their meals at the same table as their servants.

Elizabeth Fry was a leading female Quaker. She combined a great evangelistic zeal with a commitment to social issues. In particular she campaigned for a reform of the nation's prisons, which were in an unimaginable state in the nineteenth century. This campaign led to involvement with other nations' prisons from 1813 onwards. She was also involved in education and homelessness.

The Factory Reformers

This loose grouping which came together in the 1830s consisted of politicians, enlightened businessmen and evangelical Christians (principally Anglican). Initially they campaigned against child labour, but later spread their efforts to reduce the long working day for all ages, and campaigned for improved and safer working conditions. The movement originated in West Yorkshire, where it was given £40,000 by the evangelical Bradford mill owner, John Wood. Further active support came from John Fielden, the great Todmorden cotton spinner, and 'Parson Bull' of Bierley in Bradford. William Wilberforce and Lord Shaftesbury were key evangelical leaders in the movement, but the most passionate personality was that of Richard Oastler, a Conservative MP. He spoke out passionately and prophetically, using violent and inflamed rhetoric, trying to tell the nation 'what any old washer-woman could tell you, that ten hours a day is too long for any child to work.' In presenting evidence to the House of Commons in 1832 Oastler argued that the mills, factories, sweat shops and pits of Britain were actually places of 'white slavery':

> On one occasion...I was in the company of a West Indian slave master and three Bradford spinners; they brought the two systems into fair comparison, and the spinners were obliged to be silent when the slave-owner said, 'Well, I have always thought myself disgraced by being the owner of black slaves, but we never in the West Indies thought it was possible for any human being to be so cruel as to require a child of nine years old to work twelve and a half hours a day; and that, you acknowledge, is your regular practice...'

It is important to remember that Oastler and the factory reformers were opposed by Tories (and many churchmen of the day) on the basis of *laissez-faire* economics. This was the idea that the market should be left free to govern itself, that government should never interfere in the making of profits and that economic competition is always a good and positive thing. (Modern day Thatcherism was of course based on the same economic principles.) Not only the factory reformers, but others campaigning for reform of public health, housing regulations and education together proved the cruelty and insensitivity of 'the market', and that capitalism always needs to be regulated and controlled.

Unlike most Victorian philanthropists, Oastler believed in full political equality and dignity for working men, and was an active supporter of Chartism, the working-class political movement. He is rightly remembered, by a statue in Bradford town centre, as the man who brought the children out of the mills. Unfortunately Bradford today knows little about the true effectiveness of his life.

Lord Shaftesbury

Lord Shaftesbury was a Tory aristocrat with a burning evangelical faith. This faith inspired in him a genuine compassion for the poor and needy which led him actually to go himself and explore the slum conditions of East London, and the mills and factories of the North of England. He used his political power, great wealth and personal gifts in a bewildering number of movements and worthy causes. These included bringing the children out of the mills and the women out of the mines. He worked for better public health conditions, for decent hospitals for the mentally ill, for improved education for 'ragged children', for an end to the practice of child chimney-sweeps, for new futures through emigration. Describing Wilberforce and Shaftesbury together Michael Hernal writes, 'Between them they removed more human misery than any other British social reformers inside or outside Parliament.'[8]

Despite all this, however, Shaftesbury was still a paternalist, looking down on the working people, knowing and wanting what he thought was best for them. He certainly had no vision to elevate them and give them equal opportunity and dignity. He rejoiced over the failure of the Chartist movement, deeming it essential for the middle classes to remain in their place, and for the working classes to remain in theirs. His own religious experience was somewhat dour and grey; this he passed on to the evangelical movement generally, and was partially responsible for producing a grim, Sabbath-keeping style of Christianity, which was a further prohibition to working people joining the church. Nevertheless he was rightly remembered as the 'Poor Man's Earl'.

The Christian Socialists

These were a group of Anglican, middle-class intellectuals who came together in the late 1840s after the failure of Chartism. They were not socialists in the modern sense of the word; they had an awareness and concern for the social evils of society and wanted to make the church aware of and committed to doing something about these evils. In this respect they failed, as the great majority of Christians then, as now, were oblivious to such issues. Nevertheless they began a tradition of socialistic outlook within the church, which continued through the Guild of St Matthew (a high-church group) in the 1870s, and William Temple in the twentieth century.

The group was led by F. D. Maurice, an inspirational teacher, preacher and prophetic figure. Other prominent members included J. M. Ludlow, Vansittart Neale, and Charles Kingsley, the popular writer. Kingsley had written *The Water Babies* to expose the evils of child labour. He went on to write a very powerful tract *Cheap Clothes and Nasty* and the novel *Alton Locke* to open up to public view the horrendous conditions in the tailoring sweat shops of East London.

The Christian Socialists produced several practical schemes, co-operatives, night schools and colleges for working-class men. These met with varying degrees of success for a while but eventually collapsed. They introduced various legal reforms through Parliament which paved the way for the progress of the co-operative and trades union movements in the second half of the century.

Maurice's goal had been to 'Christianise the Socialists, and to Socialise the Christians.' This was only ever partially achieved. In the late nineteenth and early twentieth centuries many socialists became increasingly frustrated and disillusioned with the church. Socialism in Britain had always had strong links with Christianity, but it was becoming an increasingly secularised movement.

Florence Nightingale

From 1844, through the middle decades of the nineteenth century, Florence Nightingale was active in hospital visiting, nursing standards and hospital reform. Inspired by her faith, she committed her life to improvements which ultimately brought relief to thousands. The best of her energy and zeal was given to the military hospitals during the Crimean War. She was also interested in hospital and sanitary conditions in India.

Thomas Barnardo

Barnardo was converted in 1862 and joined the Plymouth Brethren. He came to London in 1866 wanting to be a missionary doctor. Once there he was deeply moved by the mass of child destitution in the East End. He opened his first home for boys in 1870. Though a powerful autocrat, he had huge reserves of energy and journalistic skills which he used to try and open the eyes of the middle classes. In 1876 he built a whole village at Ilford for his children. By the time of his death in 1905, he had admitted 59,384 children to his homes, helped 20,000 to emigrate and given some material help to a further 250,000.

George Lansbury

Born in 1859, Lansbury eventually established himself firmly in the East End of London, where he was a much loved character, being known as the 'John Bull of Bow'. He was a committed socialist, eventually rising to be leader of the Labour Party in opposition in the early 1930s. Lansbury was one of the most respected and most genuinely loved politicians of the twentieth century. He committed his life to pacifism, votes for women and the needs and deprivations of the working classes. His socialism, however, came not from Marx but from the Bible. Unlike most socialist Christians in the twentieth century, he was not Methodist but Anglican. George Lansbury died in 1940.

William Temple

Born in 1881, Temple came to prominence in the 1920s. He is perhaps the ultimate example of a high-ranking Anglican placing the concerns of the 'social gospel' alongside those of evangelism and church unity. As Bishop of Manchester, York and finally Canterbury, his concerns for the poor and needy, and for peace, justice and social righteousness were paramount. His preaching and writing had a huge impact on the church of his day. Unfortunately Temple died while still relatively young in 1944, and his impact on the church and on society were cut short.

This all too brief list represents just the better known names of a long list of Christian men and women who have tried to live out the prophetic hunger for justice and the gospel life of compassion in a hard industrial society. The society in which they lived, and even the church of which they were members, never really accepted their example.

Notes

1. J. Obelkevich, *Religion and Rural Society: South Lindsey 1825–75* (Clarendon Press: Oxford, 1976).
2. E. P. Thompson, *The Making of the English Working Classes* (Pelican: 1963), Ch. 11.
3. A. D. Gilbert, *Religion and Society in Industrial England* (Longman: Harlow, 1976).
4. E. R. Wickham, *Church and People in an Industrial City* (1957).
5. P. Joyce, *Work, Society and Politics* (Harvester Press: Brighton, 1980).
6. K. S. Inglis, *Churches and the Working Classes in Victorian England* (Routledge & Kegan Paul: 1963).
7. J. H. Davies, *Baptised by Fire* (Hodder & Stoughton: 1987).
8. Michael Hennell, *Sons of the Prophets* (SPCK: London, 1979).

CHAPTER THREE

A CHRISTIAN PERSPECTIVE ON THE CLASS STRUGGLE

There are always big difficulties in discussing class. The terms 'upper class', 'middle class', and 'working class' are all huge generalisations. There are groups and sub-groups within each of these classifications. There are some people in the working class who earn more money than some in the middle class. There are lots of individuals who defy classification, who seem to overlap classes, or hover between them. Nevertheless, the basic terms are still useful if we think of them only as generalisations and if we use them as a fairly simple guide to understanding. Christians in particular are usually very unhappy talking about social class, class division and the class struggle. Such talk seems to be divisive. It seems to be all about violence and money, very Marxist and nothing to do with the Bible. Much of this fear of class-struggle language is in fact due to spiritual immaturity and the desire to hide our heads in the sand and avoid the real world. When we take our heads out of the sand, and breathe a few deep lungsful of real truth, we realise that our world, our country, even our town is torn in two between the rich and the poor. We know that this inequality is unfair; we do not believe that it was ever part of God's plan that some people should have a huge slice of life's cake while others have just a few crumbs. As soon as we begin to think such thoughts we are accepting the reality of social

51

class division. Marx does indeed talk a lot about class conflict, but that doesn't mean Christians have to avoid it; in fact Christians were talking, thinking and praying about such things long before Marx.

The Bible and social class

The Church of England has traditionally been conservative in every aspect of its life, and certainly in its politics. Evangelicals of all denominations have, during the twentieth century, been trained to distrust and reject anything remotely left-wing. So it is not surprising when we find the majority of Christians and particularly the evangelical/charismatic group skirting around such areas as social class and injustice. The Bible, by contrast, ploughs straight to the heart of the matter. Thus we have the great covenant commandments of Leviticus and Deuteronomy, attempting to protect the poor from the rich. We have the stories, graphically told, of David and Bathsheba, and Ahab and Naboth's vineyard, stories of the 'rich and powerful' wanting what God had promised to lesser men.

There are the great prophetic denunciations of Amos against the class-ridden society of his day. In the gospels we see Jesus on numerous occasions drawing attention to the rich and poor divide, and bringing in a kingdom which had particular good news for the poor and 'woes' for the rich. Throughout the New Testament there are warnings against 'love of wealth', while the letter of James again addresses the evils of class structure. Finally, the whole evil system is brought crashing down in judgement in Revelation.

Thinking and talking about class isn't wrong or un-Christian. What is wrong and evil is the class structure itself, with all the pain and suffering that it brings. The best way we as Christians can serve this kingdom of Mammon and help preserve it is by keeping silent about it and pretending it isn't there, or that it is nothing to do with the gospel. This is not the Christian way; ours is the way of the kingdom, which is God's rule breaking into this world to end pain, darkness, sin and injustice wherever it prevails.

Social class

The idea of social class implies that society, which is basically the great human mass of all the millions of people living in Britain, can be divided into several layers, and can be pictured as taking the shape of a pyramid. The theory goes that the people at the top of the pyramid, be they aristocratic landowners, self-made industrialists, or smoothly operating developers are the upper classes. They own most of the land, most of the factories, shops, companies and even most of the money itself. They live in the biggest houses, eat the best food and get the highest quality of education and medicine, etc. All these commodities are limited and there is not enough for everyone to have lots of everything (though there is enough for everyone to have sufficient). If some people are going to have lots of the very best then some others are going to have to go without. Thus at the bottom of the pyramid there is a much larger number of people, the lower classes. They do not own land and factories, etc; all they own is their own labour and human ability. When they work they eat, when they cannot offer their labour due to ill health, old age or mass unemployment, they go hungry.

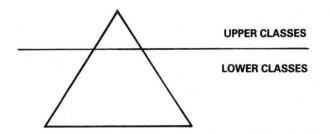

In between the two sections of the human pyramid there is a

third layer, the middle classes. The middle classes have particularly useful labour and gifts, they are doctors and teachers and other such professionals. They are often employed by the upper classes to maintain, increase and administer their wealth, as bank managers, solicitors or stockbrokers. They often possess reasonable amounts of wealth themselves, and are valuable as managers of the lower classes.

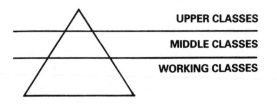

Thus the pyramid came to have three layers. The churches have been keen to meet the spiritual needs of, and to give active support to the top two layers of the pyramid. Thus the Church of England has traditionally belonged to the upper classes; Independents (Congregationalists, Baptists and Quakers, etc) have looked after the middle classes, while Methodism started out among the upper working and lower middle classes, and gradually clawed its way upwards. These layers are not completely watertight compartments; poor people sometimes acquire education and move up the pyramid. While the wealthy occasionally experience financial disaster and decline and drop down the ladder, this sort of equalling-out movement does not happen nearly as often as we are told it does by the defenders of the pyramid. Furthermore, the lines between the social layers are blurred, so that between lower and middle classes there is actually a zone of lower middle class and higher working class. These people are often skilled tradesmen, foremen, shopkeepers, lower-grade clerical workers and small-scale business people. Since the Second

World War this group or band has massively expanded to the extent that it has changed the basic shape of the pyramid.

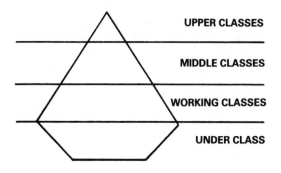

Today the lower classes are increasingly referred to as an 'underclass'. Each day they struggle to make ends meet, each night they watch glossy TV commercials reminding them of what everyone else is enjoying and what they cannot have. The underclass is not a handful of people, it is a huge group number-ing millions, often unnoticed by the majority of us, usually outside the life and range of the Christian church, constantly maligned by the tabloid press, written off as beer-guzzling, fag-smoking, bingo-playing, welfare-state-cheating idlers. Yet they are specially loved and valued by God their Father.

Class conflict

Injustice

Class conflict (sometimes referred to as the class war) grows out of the injustice of the class structure.

The implication of the creation story of Genesis is that God has provided enough for everyone: enough land, enough food, enough of all the good things of life. This implication is rein-forced in Genesis 9 where, after the great flood, God promises material prosperity to Noah and all his descendants. Clearly it is God's will for all of us to have a reasonable slice of the rich creation cake. Yet we live alongside many people who see precious little of such things. The sense of 'natural justice' in all of us would suggest that those who hold most of creation's wealth share it with those who hold the least. This sense of natural justice has been planted there by God and is in fact an outworking of his divine justice. God's sense of justice is revolted by man's class structures of greed and inequality. When we study his word carefully with an open mind, we find that biblical justice fatally condemns these man-made divisions.

> Blessed are you who are poor,
>   for yours is the kingdom of God.
> Blessed are you who hunger now,
>   for you will be satisfied.
> Blessed are you who weep now,
>   for you will laugh.
>
> Luke 6:20-21

> But woe to you who are rich,
>   for you have already received your comfort.
> Woe to you who are well fed now,
>   for you will go hungry.
> Woe to you who laugh now,
>   for you will mourn and weep.
>
> Luke 6:24-25

It is these divisions which create a world of the 'haves' and the 'have-nots'.

Richard Oastler in the first half of the nineteenth century, was particularly enraged by the great evil of the system, and expressed his feelings in a very powerful way.

> I never see one of these pious, canting, murdering, 'liberal', 'respectable' saints, riding in his carriage, but I remember that the vehicle is built of infants' bones; that it is lined with their skins; that the tassels

are made of their hair; the traces and harness of their sinews; and that the very oil, with which the wheels are greased, is made of Infants' Blood! (quoted in Hopkins, op cit, p 60).

Many Christians today could find this language rather offensive; in fact it is very similar to that of the prophet Micah (Mic 3:1–3).

Conflict

The conflict arises out of the pain, distrust and bitterness which exists between the 'haves' and the 'have-nots'. The poor argue, organise strikes, marches and protests, and sometimes fight for their fair share of what has been given by God to all people. Contrary to what people often believe, the English working classes have been extraordinarily passive, patient and peaceful in their struggle. Most of the bloodshed has actually been caused by over-hasty and aggressive politicians, industrialists and police-men.

This has been the painful experience of working-class activists in Bradford, Manchester, the East End of London, South Wales, etc, throughout the nineteenth and twentieth centuries. Most of such spilt blood has flowed from the veins of the already exploited poorer people. Many people will be unhappy with this contention, yet there are numerous historical incidents to back it up; eg the use of the army in the nineteenth century, and the Metropolitan Police force in the early twentieth century, to break the strikes of starving miners in South Wales. Similarly peaceful hunger marches during the depression were turned into violent confrontations by State force.

The upper classes are the 'haves', which in the context of the class conflict has usually included a good many of the middle classes. They are determined to hang on to everything they own, and in some cases have actually convinced themselves that their privileged position is somehow right and ordained by God. Their position and wealth gives them great power. They use the power of industry, with threats of unemployment, loss of housing, etc.

They usually control government which passes laws and employs police forces and armies which can be deployed against the lower classes. They control the mass media (in fact today they own virtually all the mass media, while the one major exception, the BBC, seems to be purposefully weakened and broken by the government. They even manage to buy control of the church (this happened in the case of Old Testament Israel, where the priests and prophets were literally bought).

There has often been a third force in the struggle, occupying a middle ground. This middle way has often contained renegades from the upper classes who have become champions of the poor. Isaiah, the Old Testament prophet, is such a person. The great strength of this grouping has usually come from the middle classes producing writers, social reformers, religious leaders and politicians. This grouping has generally rejected the worst excesses of the class system, but rarely gone over completely to the cause of the poor.

From the Industrial Revolution to the present day the class conflict can be traced through numerous incidents, confrontations and tragedies of our social history. A few of these are indicated in the paragraphs below.

The Luddites became active in the late eighteenth century although it was not until the nineteenth century that they came to be known as Luddites. Their main influence was in the predominantly textile areas (West Riding, Manchester, Nottingham). New inventions and machinery had been introduced. Contrary to the popular image the Luddites were not so much opposed to the new inventions as to the way they were used to give even bigger profits to the manufacturers and to cause widespread destitution among the workers. The government used spies, informers and a bigger army than was employed against Napoleon, but never actually asked the Luddites about the nature of their grievances. Innocent men were wrongly accused, some being transported, others hanged.

The Peterloo Massacre involved a peaceful mass meeting of

60,000 people, held in Manchester in 1819, calling for political reform. The local yeomanry charged the crowd, killing 11 and injuring 400.

The Great Reform Act of 1832 was a typical example of the action of the middle classes. The working classes had worked with the middle classes for the right to vote to be extended; in the end it was the middle classes who got the vote and then deserted their allies.

In 1834 came the case of the Tolpuddle Martyrs. The then Home Secretary, Lord Melbourne, wanting to make an example of unionism, attacked six labourers in Dorset. Despite the fact that their union membership pledged them to non-violence, they were transported. There was a strong public reaction and they were brought home in 1836.

Chartism was the first truly mass working-class political movement: it represented a campaign for democracy for the whole nation involving all classes. At its height, it commanded the support of millions, who met at huge open-air gatherings. Bradford was one of the country's strongest Chartist areas. Although it aimed at being a peaceful movement, there were often small outbreaks of violence on its fringes. Thus in Bradford there was a riot in 1837; an attempted insurrection in 1840; and large-scale marches in the Queensbury, Halifax and Great Horton areas, and in the Bingley and East Morton areas in 1842. These marches closed down various mills and involved some violence. The Chartists in Bradford were generally supported by a group of nonconformist Liberals, including at one stage Titus Salt. They were strongly opposed by a balancing group of Anglican Tories.

New Unionism arose in the later years. In the early nineteenth century, the unions had been the preserve of the skilled workers, exclusive and relatively small. In the second half of the century the labouring millions began organising their own mass-membership unions. Fighting for decent living conditions, healthy workplaces and wages to lift them above the level of poverty, they had some victories, but many painful defeats.

There has been a long tradition of gifted novelists, who have used their art to highlight the evils of poverty, and to expose the tyrants. This literary tradition was particularly strong in the nineteenth and early twentieth centuries and included such writers as George Eliot, Thomas Hardy, Charles Kingsley, Elizabeth Gaskell and even Benjamin Disraeli, a Conservative Prime Minister. Most famous of all was Charles Dickens. Victorian England was very proud of its great industries, cities and commercial success. Dickens, in his novels, continually confronted the Victorians with pictures of the victims of their success. On one occasion he referred to the Tories as a 'ruthless set of bloody-minded villains bearing down all before them with ruffianly barbarity and brutal violence'.[1]

Not all such writers, however, came from a middle-class background. Robert Tressell, who wrote the *Ragged Trousered Philanthropists*, Arthur Morrison, author of *A Child of the Jago*, and Walter Greenwood who captured the feel of life in Salford during the Depression so movingly in *Love on the Dole*, were all men writing from out of the situation they were describing. Their books are full of anger and tears and have a particular importance to Christians.

From the turn of the century onwards the struggle between the classes continued. The Independent Labour Party was set up in Bradford in 1893 and led to the present Labour Party being established in 1900 under the leadership of Keir Hardie. Ramsay Macdonald was its first Prime Minister, but he is often seen as a virtual traitor to the cause, leading a national coalition which reduced dole money and introduced a means test. Hardie, Macdonald and many of the early leaders and activists came out of the churches, disillusioned at their lack of concern for working people. Keir Hardie spoke these words to a Congregationalist gathering in 1897: 'The reason the Labour Party has turned its back on the church was because the church had turned its back upon them.'[2]

The Depression was a period of especially hard poverty and

unemployment in the early nineteen-thirties. The country as a whole was actually growing in prosperity and average wages were going up, but in the old industrial areas there was great suffering. The dreaded means test was introduced. The people marched (peacefully) and the police were used to break them up.

One little-known minor skirmish in this long-drawn-out class struggle was the 1932 Kinder Trespass. This one incident, however, encapsulates many of the essential elements of the struggle.

Rambling and cycling had become favourite working-class pastimes in the late twenties and thirties. Thousands of young people trapped in the grimy factories and shabby houses of Manchester, Sheffield and the West Riding escaped at weekends onto the Pennine Moors. Huge areas of these moorlands, however, were held as a private property and enjoyed by a tiny handful of grouse shooters. The problem was particularly acute in the Peak district, where the public had access to 1,212 acres while 109,500 acres were held by landowners. Hundreds of young people assembled for a mass protest on 24th April in defiance of police and gamekeepers. Their protest was peaceful; they were not asking for anything revolutionary, merely the freedom to enjoy the countryside of their native land, which they believed was a basic right (which we all today take for granted). The full power of the press and the police and a very twisted trial conducted before a highly prejudiced judge and jury resulted in prison sentences of up to six months for the leaders of the ramblers.

Today we enjoy the freedom and beauty of the National Parks. Christians like to think of the countryside as a gift from God, not to rich landowners, but to all people as a place where all can go and often feel specially close to God. Yet without the Kinder Trespass and the other mass rambles that it inspired, there would probably be no National Parks.

The post-war Labour government introduced the Health Service and the Welfare State generally. Many would say that this is the only truly socialist government the country has ever had, and that the benefits for the working classes were immense. However, the 1970s and 1980s saw a severe shift to the right. The gap between rich and poor widened, and there was greater prosperity for some but poverty for many. The Welfare State was seen as the 'nanny state' and was subsequently weakened. Local and national democracy became increasingly distorted. The means test is set to be recalled under the new title of 'benefit targetting'.

These are only the major incidents in a long-drawn-out struggle. Over the last 200 years the lower classes have been given hardly anything. What they have achieved in terms of decent working conditions, wages, political rights and freedoms, has had to be fought for. There has been suffering, misuse of law and the forces of order, and bloodshed throughout the industrial regions, especially South Wales, Yorkshire and the North East, and even in rural settings such as Kent and the Forest of Dean.

Throughout the long struggle there have been many individual Christians who have stood alongside the poor. Shaftesbury, F. D. Maurice and Keir Hardie are three particularly well-remembered ones, but there are many who have been equally compassionate and equally committed who are less well-known. The church as an institution, however, almost always chose either to sit on the fence or to support the establishment, in effect siding with the rich against the poor.

Summary: The Irrelevant Church and its History

1. The nineteenth century displayed a huge gulf between rich and poor. The rich were very rich and the poor were very poor. Their accommodation, working conditions, health, diet and general quality of life were of an almost sub-human standard. This rich/poor divide was established on the back of the class system. Capitalistic industry was its driving force.

    Far from opposing this system, the churches (especially the protestant churches) actually supported and buttressed it. In so doing they patronised, manipulated and deserted the lower classes.

Class, capitalism and the rich/poor divide are all still with us. And the church? Well, we are still here, too. In the past the church has made some wrong choices; what sort of choices are we making today? Such choices are not primarily about politics. They are about compassion, justice and truth.

2. The last century produced a courageous, angry and deeply loving number of men and women. Working in groups or as individuals they went against the prevailing culture of church and society. They stood out, and actually changed things. Where are the Wilberforces, the Frys, the Lansburys of today, and if and when they appear, do they get our support?

3. The nineteenth century church allowed itself to be captured by the prevailing class structure. The upper and middle classes ruled and administered there just as they did everywhere. The lower classes were tolerated, smiled upon, and seen as worthy targets for the charitable. A truly working class style of worship, church life, leadership and evangelism was never really allowed to develop. This poses some critical questions about the church today. A middle class church is irrelevant to working class people.

4. The three great strands of the English church each went through periods of numerical growth, which included some partial growth in working class areas. We can register this growth and summarise the main factors that helped produce it:

Anglicanism   —A four-fold increase was witnessed in the second half of the century. This was due mainly to structural reorganisation, building of new churches, renewal of the clergy and a huge emphasis on evangelism.

Non-conformity —The various non-conformist churches experienced anything between a six- and nine-fold increase during the latter decades of the eighteenth and the early ones of the nineteenth centuries. Such growth was produced by 'revivalism' especially in rural and semi-rural areas, and by the use of populist techniques and local working class preachers.

Roman Catholicism—The Roman Catholics enjoyed a huge twenty-fold increase spread across the century. However, it must be remembered that they started out from a very small base. Irish immigration and good pastoral practices made such growth possible.

The growth came when there was the urgency, flexibility and faith in the churches. Unfortunately, it was followed by institutionalisation, stagnation and inevitable decline. The Primitive Methodists and Salvation Army are particularly clear examples of this process.

If we today have a desire to see the church become relevant and grow, then there are good practices here to encourage and guide us, and bad mistakes that must not be repeated.

Notes

1. Quoted in *Dickens: A Biography* by Fren Kaplan (Hodder and Stoughton: London, 1988).
2. Quoted in K. S. Inglis, *Churches and the Working Classes in Victorian England* (Routledge and Kegan Paul: 1963), p 297.

Part II

*The Irrelevant Church
and the Bible*

CHAPTER FOUR

WEALTH AND POVERTY IN THE BIBLE

Trying to discover the Bible's teaching on wealth and poverty is like trying to follow a road through a busy town centre. At some points the road is very clear, eg in the law codes of Deuteronomy, in many of the chapters of Psalms and Proverbs, in the eighth-century prophets, in the Gospels and in the Epistle of James in the New Testament. Elsewhere the road seems to disappear into all the other themes and subjects of biblical teaching. Nevertheless, with attention to detail and much patience, it is possible to see and stay on the road right through the Bible.

The task is made more difficult by the fact that what we have so far been thinking of as a single road, seems to become, on closer inspection, a whole series of roads. The first road or biblical theme to emerge is the idea that worldly prosperity is a sign of God's blessing. Later on in the Old Testament another road seems to cut right across this first one, as the question is repeatedly asked 'Why do the wicked prosper?'. Other minor roads appear to give warnings to the rich; advice to the stingy; encouragement to the charitable; and comfort to the poverty-stricken. An important road which is particularly clear in the New Testament leads in the direction of shared possessions and of church communities where class and financial status have no power. The major and dominant road begins with the Israelites settling in the Promised Land and goes right through to the Book of Revelation. It concerns the rampant exploitation by which the poor have been stripped of what God gave them. They have been stripped by the rich and powerful. The poor have been denied human justice but they are the recipients of special divine love.

Before beginning the journey, however, it is important to make a vital introductory remark. Most of us come to the Bible with our lives and minds already dressed up in lots of attitudes, opinions and ideas (I certainly include myself in this). These we have picked up along the way, from our parents, from our schooling, from odd things we have read in magazines or heard in pubs, information gleaned from the TV, prejudices dictated to us by our newspapers.

When it comes to issues of money, our attitudes and opinions are particularly strong on two counts. Firstly, in terms of individual morality, how much money should I have? How do I get it? What should I spend it on? How much should I give away? How important is it to me anyway? Secondly, there are corporate or community issues. How should money, resources, work, etc be shared out? Who gets the most and why? How do we avoid financial corruption? This is the area of politics and most of us have strong political feelings.

In fact, our opinions can be so strong that we merely pick out one or two verses and in so doing we twist and use the Bible to back up our prejudice, rather than allowing it to speak the truth to us. Writing about the need for the Bible to have a real impact on our attitudes, Gutierrez observed

> Moreover we must not forget that the word of God issues its challenges. The scriptures are not a passive store of answers to our questions. We indeed read the Bible, but we can also say that the Bible 'reads us.'[1]

For the Christian the Bible represents God's opinions about life. In trying to discover and follow the route through the Bible on the issues of wealth and poverty, we are trying to discover and follow the mind of God. We come to the Bible fully dressed in our own attitudes and ways of thinking. We have to be willing to put these aside and to stand naked before God's word, and then to redress our minds and lives with the ideas and beliefs that come out of that word.

The historical background

To understand fully any piece of biblical teaching we have to understand its historical background, before we can appreciate the various aspects of that teaching in their full context. For instance, we cannot fully understand Amos's words on the summer and winter houses of the rich until we know something of the social divide between rich and poor in eighth-century Israel. Similarly, Paul's words about slaves and freemen being 'one in Christ' lack their full power until we learn something about the institution of slavery in Paul's day. However, the Bible covers a very long period of history, from virtually the earliest Middle-Eastern civilisation right up to the Roman Empire. Throughout this period, social, political and economic situations were changing. For simplicity's sake we can divide this constantly changing process into four major periods. So our road takes us through not one historical landscape, but through four.

1. The tribal—nomadic period, 2200–1400 BC (approx)
   This period begins with Abraham and stretches right through to the wilderness wanderings of Moses. The Israelites were nomads, and their wealth was held by the tribe, not by individuals. The covenant was established in this period.

2. The settled agricultural period, 1400–1000 BC (approx)
   Settlement in the Promised Land led to the early phase of the monarchy. The Israelites became farmers, each with their own piece of private property. This was the dawn of what later generations would term capitalism, with a gap appearing for the first time between rich and poor. The biblical books of Joshua, Judges, Ruth, 1 Samuel and 1 Chronicles are all set in this period.

3. The centralised state period, 1000–586 BC

Israel had been a collection of tribal areas, but these areas lost much of their independence as power, wealth and religion were centralised around the monarchy, the capital city, the army and the civil service, etc. The kingdom was divided into two, with the northern capital of Samaria falling to the Assyrians in 722, and the southern one, Judea, being taken by the Babylonians in 586.

The great biblical prophets, Isaiah, Jeremiah, Amos, etc have to be read against this background, as do the warnings to the rich, and the messianic notions of kingship found in Psalms and Proverbs.

4. The imperial subjection period, 586 BC–AD 100

For almost all the rest of biblical history, God's people were part of someone else's empire: Babylonian, Persian, Greek or Roman. Taxes were imposed, alien institutions and customs were introduced. The gap between rich and poor continued to widen.

Jesus entered this historical landscape and established his church, based on a renewal and expansion of covenant principles and prophetic traditions. This period will be considered in Chapter 5, The New Testament.

The tribal-nomadic period

Patriarchal prosperity

The patriarchs, the fathers of Israel, originated from one of the world's first great civilisations. Abraham came from Ur of the Chaldeans, probably situated on the Euphrates in today's southern Iraq. Marching with his animals, possessions and extended family, he was probably part of an extensive migration from the East to the West of the ancient world.

They lived as large families or tribes; parents, children, brothers and sisters, even servants and slaves would all have been part of the one closely woven unit. The patriarchs and the later Israelites, who followed Moses in the wilderness, have traditionally been thought of as typical Middle-Eastern nomads. In fact, recent scholarship describes them more as 'semi-nomads' combining a fairly settled agricultural existence with that of being wandering keepers of herds and flocks. Thus Jacob is seen as giving Esau a gift of forty cows and ten bulls, animals which were domesticated by settled agriculturalists rather than nomads, who by contrast kept sheep and goats. Similarly, the early part of the story of Joseph and his brothers shows them being involved not only in the tending of flocks, but also in the binding of sheaves. These semi-nomads of the patriarchal and wilderness periods probably practised transhumance, ie moving their animals back and forth on a seasonal basis. They lived on the edge of towns and cities and there would have been a strong interplay between the two communities. For instance, it seems that in certain areas a semi-nomadic community may have moved their animals out to graze in the wilderness during and after the rainy season, and as the pastures were gradually worn out they would have returned to pasture in the stubble of the town's harvested fields, offering free fertilisation in exchange for free access. Being described by themselves and others as aliens in someone else's land, they were not particularly interested in land (apart from acquiring burial sites) or private property (both of which concepts are held as virtually sacred in our world). Their wealth was made up of herds, flocks, servants and treasure, and all belonged to the family or tribe, not certain individuals. At certain times this wealth was considerable; 'Abram had become very wealthy in livestock and in silver and gold' (Gen 13:2). In fact, they had so many animals at this stage that they had to divide into two, with one half going under Lot's leadership.

Their wealth was accumulated through various channels. Hard work and skilful management of resources was clearly part of Jacob's success (Gen 30). Gifts, marriage settlements, war booty and deals were other sources. Even that which came through falsity, eg Abraham and Pharaoh (Gen 12) and Abimelech (Gen 20), and even through open dishonesty (Jacob's cheating of Laban), seems to have been accepted without question or scruple.

In Summary

Underlying this lifestyle are two fundamental socio-economic principles.

1. All wealth is shared wealth. It is not private, but belongs to the community. There is no suggestion of division between rich and poor. When the people are poor, they are all poor; when rich they are all rich.
2. All wealth is ultimately attributed to God. He is the great provider. Thus their property is an indication of God's blessing. So when Laban sees the valuable gold trinkets that Abraham's servant is able to offer to Rebekah his sister, his response is, 'You are blessed by the Lord' (Gen 24:31). The same servant later on attributes his master's wealth to God's blessing (Gen 24:35). Two generations later, Joseph's prosperity is similarly attributed to God (Gen 39:2).

This concept of God blessing his people with financial prosperity remained as an important aspect of the Bible's teaching on wealth and poverty.

The settled agricultural period

Settlement in Canaan

The semi-nomadic, tribal, sharing lifestyle of the Israelites was gradually transformed by their settlement in Canaan, the land flowing with milk and honey (ie a land offering all the potential for material prosperity as the fruit of hard work). This was a predominantly agricultural land of private property, farms, towns and cities, with an agricultural religion and a strong class structure of landowners, farmers and slaves, etc. The power and wealth, however, were contained in the walled cities concentrated around the small petty kingships with their bureaucrats and armed retainers.

The half-wandering, half-farming Israelites settled in the land

and became a much more stationary agricultural community. They lived in small unwalled towns and villages, and there emerged a very real tension between their lifestyle, religion and socio-economic structures and those of the city-dwelling Canaanites. Each tribe was allocated its own region and, within this, each family its own piece of land. Thus the land, which they believed belonged to God, was entrusted to them corporately. They were in effect the stewards and trustees of God's property. Inevitably this meant that to some extent they became involved in competition rather than co-operation. Some were given good land, others poor land; some were gifted farmers, others discovered themselves to be unsuited to it; some prospered while others failed.

If the system had been run according to God's principles, all would have prospered (Deut 15:4). In the real world, however, human beings tend to follow the urges of their own selfishness rather than God's sense of fairness and equality. For the first time, divisions between rich and poor began to emerge. As failure, debt and landlessness became growing problems it was necessary to have a safety-net, a protection against complete destitution and slavery. Thus a system was developed whereby a poor man could opt into slavery as a means of working off his debt and finding a decent level of material provision and poor relief. There were vital safeguards to protect the poor in this system, to recognise and give relief to the most vulnerable members of society, and there were prohibitions to prevent the capitalistic accumulation of large-scale land-ownership.

Covenant

During Israel's wilderness experience, in the latter stages of their tribal nomadic period, and as they were preparing to enter their Promised Land, a covenant had been formed between them and God. This was a binding legal agreement given to them by God in which he promised to be their providing and protecting God, and they promised to worship and belong to him and no other God.

Once they had settled in Canaan, this covenant was to be the basis of the Israelites' national life. Thus the covenant forbade them to participate in the Canaanite religion and instead to maintain their own. However, the covenant was not just about worship. It extended to every area of Israel's social, economic and community life. It introduced laws, customs and standards in an attempt to bring the full breadth of human life into line with divine life.

The foundation of the covenant was the idea that God was a righteous God and that he wanted his people to be a righteous people. Righteousness is about 'right living' and 'right values'. What is 'right' is defined by God's ways of living and his values. Righteousness bestows 'human rights', and God was defined as a God of justice. Thus, justice became fundamental to his people's community living.

With Israel living in a hard, competitive, greedy world, covenant righteousness was essential for their spiritual and moral well-being. The great law codes of the Pentateuch grew out of this situation. They are relevant, practical and humane, they are examples of how God's law holds together the sacred and the secular.

Covenant Law

Central to the great law codes of Exodus, Leviticus and Deuteronomy are the Ten Commandments (Ex 20:1–17) with the fundamental principle 'thou shalt not covet'; and the 'Book of the Covenant' (Ex 20:22—23:33). The various ordinances of the Book of the Covenant attempt to identify and give special protection to the more vulnerable members of a selfish society, eg slaves, aliens, widows, orphans and the poor; to contain and prohibit the widespread use of violence; to avoid exploitation in money-lending and employment practices; to prevent work of any kind on the Sabbath.

The Book of the Covenant also introduces the idea of the seventh year, which is developed in Deuteronomy and Leviticus into two related concepts:

1. The sabbatical year (Deut 15:1–15)
   Every seventh year the land is to lie fallow and unworked; animals and the poor should be allowed to help themselves freely to anything that thus grows freely.
       All outstanding debts should be cancelled.
       All Hebrew slaves should be set free.
2. The year of jubilee (Lev 25)
   The land of Israel is seen not to belong to the individual farmers as landowners; they are tenants, for God himself owns the land (25:23).
       As a reminder of this, and as a barrier against land-owning monopolies, every fiftieth year should see a giving back of the individual plots of land to their original owners or owners' families.
       There should also be a setting-free of Hebrew slaves, and provision to help the poor, etc.

There are also further ordinances concerning tithing the produce of the land in order to feed the poor and needy (Deut 14:29/26:12); payment of religious offerings and making of sacrifices being reduced in the case of the poor (Lev 12:8; 14:21; 27:8); making of loans to, and the employing of poor men (Deut 24:12, 14, 15); leaving the gleanings behind in harvested fields, or olive branches in the vineyard and then allowing the poor free access to them (Deut 24:19; Lev 19:19; Lev 23:22).

In Summary

Underpinning all these laws and stipulations is the painful realisation that in a society of rich and poor, it is always the poor who will suffer. The gap will get wider, injustice will flourish and exploitation will be the order of the day, all of which is a denial of covenant righteousness. Covenant law was a vain attempt to contain, reduce and limit some of the injustice.

The ironic and painful truth behind all this was that there need not have been any poor in the Promised Land; there was enough blessing for all (Deut 15:4). God's original covenant vision had been that all his people might prosper together (Deut 5:33; 29:9).

The centralised state

The books of Joshua and Judges paint the picture of Israel's early life in their new land: a loosely united collection of tribes, living independently of each other but coming together when an outside enemy challenged. The threat posed by Philistine aggression in the second half of the eleventh century was by far the greatest danger that Israel ever faced during this period; it threatened the very existence, not just of one or two tribal areas, but of the whole of Israel. In the face of this aggression the people asked Samuel, their great religious leader, to give them a king. Such a move towards a central monarchy went very much against the grain of Israel's traditions. Samuel's discourse with God on the subject (1 Sam 8:6–22) shows that the people's demand for a king was in effect a rejection of God's kingship over them, and of the special arrangements by which Israel was called to have different values and social and economic structures from those of surrounding nations. Samuel went on to warn the people that a monarchy would mean a centralised government, excesses of affluence and poverty and much social injustice. The people refused to listen, and Samuel's words were to be painfully and prophetically true through the remainder of their history.

Saul was the first king, but his was a very simple style of rule. It was David who really established the monarchy, created the capital city of Jerusalem, set up a large court, a professional army, a full-time civil service, etc, all of which had to be paid for by taxation. Solomon carried on this process of centralising power, influence and wealth and augmented this with the building of the Jerusalem Temple, thus centralising the nation's religious life too.

Israel evolved from being a loose tribal grouping to become a centralised nation-state, with great extremes of wealth and poverty. The caring, sharing nation of early Israel was distorted into a harsh, primitive type of capitalistic kingdom. This state was torn in two on Solomon's death, with a northern kingdom of ten tribes gathered around their own king, and capital city Samaria, called Israel. The two remaining southern tribes continued as the much-reduced state of Judah.

Decadence

There followed a long period of prosperity for both north and south. There were occasional local wars and internal coups as kings were from time to time replaced. Throughout this period, however, trade and commerce were sound and provided much wealth, most of which ended up in the pockets of the rich. The gap between the poor masses and the affluent elite widened, while injustice and exploitation increased. Two incidents vividly illustrate these social and economic trends.

Excavations in Tirzah (Tell el-Farah) show housing in the tenth century BC to be roughly all of the same standard. By the eighth century, however, there were large houses of the rich concentrated in certain neighbourhoods, while smaller, poorer houses were squeezed into slum areas. The 'one people' had physically divided into two.

A second example is the story of Ahab's stealing of Naboth's vineyard (1 Kings 21), which is set in the mid ninth century. It shows Ahab abusing his position as king to acquire Naboth's freehold. In earlier days, when every Israelite saw himself as a freeborn son of Abraham, with his own God-given piece of land, such a practice would have been unthinkable.

Denunciation

With Israel sinking into this cruel 'rich and poor' lifestyle, the great prophets burst onto the stage. Their denunciations represented the moral and religious conscience of God as they made their demands for a return to Israel's true God, and a giving up of the worship of false gods; a trusting in the covenant promises of God for national security, rather than in the strength of their, or anyone else's armies; an establishing of justice for the poor, needy and oppressed; and a fairer distribution of national wealth.

Our theme of wealth and poverty leads us to consider in particular the issues raised in the latter two of these areas. The prophet Amos led Hosea, Micah, Jeremiah, Isaiah and Ezekiel, etc in a furious attack on the rich and powerful: 'They sell...the needy for a pair of sandals. They trample on the heads of the poor as upon the dust of the ground' (Amos 2:6, 7).

The rich have extravagant lifestyles with large houses (Amos 3:15; Is 3:14), fabulous furnishings (Amos 6:4), lavish food and drink (Amos 6:4, 5) and arrogant and powerful wives (Amos 4:1). Yet they are still covetous: 'They covet fields and seize them, and houses, and take them' (Micah 2:2), and 'they devour the poor in their greed.

> You who tear the skin from my people and the flesh from their bones; who eat my people's flesh, strip off their skin and break their bones in pieces; who chop them up like meat for the pan, like flesh for the pot (Micah 3:2–3).

The rich are fat and greasy (Jer 5:28) and capitalistic (Is 5:8). Their greed has destroyed any semblance of justice: 'You who turn justice into bitterness and cast righteousness to the ground' (Amos 5:7). Open bribery is prevalent in the courts (Amos 5:12–13; Micah 7:3); false scales and cheating are common in the marketplace (Micah 6:11; Amos 8:5). Laws and decrees are produced, not to protect the most vulnerable people in society, but actually to deprive and oppress them (Is 10:1–4).

Religion which ignores such social ills is empty and blasphemous: 'I hate, I despise your religious feasts; I cannot stand your assemblies' (Amos 5:21). 'Away with the noise of your songs! I will not listen to the music of your harps. But let justice roll on like a river, righteousness like a never-failing stream!' (Amos 5:23, 24).

The people cannot wait for their times of worship to finish, so that they can return to their extortion (Amos 8:5). Often the rich are vigilant in their worship and fasting, but this is not what God wants: 'Yet on the day of your fasting, you do as you please, and exploit all your workers' (Is 58:3). 'Is not this the kind of fasting I have chosen: to loose the chains of injustice and untie the cords of the yoke' (Is 58:6).

The priests and prophets, leaders and elders are all involved: they have been bought (Mic 3:11; Jer 8:10). They are a bunch of beer-sodden drunkards (Is 28:7), who grind down the poor and plunder their houses (Is 3:14–15).

The prophets and the covenant

The prophets were not revolutionaries, introducing new ideas and aims; in fact they were traditionalists. They were attempting to take people back to the traditions of the covenant and to remind them of its ideas about justice, social righteousness, equality, and protection of the most vulnerable people in society. The essence of the covenant was that sacred and secular (ie what a person does on the Sabbath and what they do in the rest of the week) are part of the same experience of being God's people.

Looking to the future, the prophets predicted that just as night follows day, so the long days of false religion and social evil would be followed by an even longer night of God's judgement. The coming judgement would represent God's rejection of their lifestyle, and would take the form of war and national disaster. Such prophecies were fulfilled, with the fall of Samaria to the Assyrians in 722 BC, and of Jerusalem to the Babylonians in 585 BC.

Judgement, however, was not to be the final word. Looking beyond this immediate horizon of national disaster, the prophetic vision saw a new day of restoration, of God in his love rebuilding the people of Israel. Two important ideas emerge out of this prophetic theology of judgement and restoration, which are of particular importance to our theme: the poor, and the Messiah.

The poor came to be viewed as a special grouping of people; they were the humble and meek. They were despised and brutalised by the rulers of this world, but would receive a special love and consolation from God (Is 58:6–10). He is to be their refuge (Is 25:4), extending to his 'afflicted ones' a particular comfort (Is 49:13). He will rescue them (Jer 20:13) and then bring down their rich and powerful oppressors (Is 26:5).

As the recipients of this special divine love and blessing, the poor are elevated into a special relationship (Is 29:19; 57:13).

The Messiah is to be the main agent of this restoration. He is God's special servant, a futuristic kingly figure, and among all his other attributes, he will have a special concern for the poor. 'With justice he will give decisions for the poor of the earth' (Is 11:4). 'The Spirit of the Sovereign Lord is on me, because the Lord has anointed me to preach good news to the poor' (Is 61:1).

Both these ideas of the meek and humble, and of the Messiah, are taken up, extended and developed in the poetry of the wisdom literature and in the New Testament's account of the life, work and teaching of Jesus.

In Summary

The prophets hated the open sinfulness of greedy Israel; they looked back to the God-given, but man-rejected, values of the covenant, and they looked forward to judgement and to restoration bringing special blessing to the poor.

Wisdom, wealth and wickedness

The covenant/prophetic tradition represents the major line of biblical teaching on wealth and poverty. This line is at the heart of the Scriptures and reaches its peak in the life and teaching of Jesus.

A second line or thread, however, can be found in what is known as the Wisdom Literature of Israel. In the Bible this is represented by the books of Job, Psalms, Proverbs and Ecclesiastes. This literature originated in courtly circles and is favourable to (though at certain points critical of) that background. It is more concerned with private religion and morality, than with the public and corporate arena of the prophets. There are some strong similarities to be found between it and the prophets (especially in the Psalms), but there are also strong differences. The two traditions have to be held in parallel; to some extent they balance each other, though not completely.

Wealth and prosperity

As in the time of the patriarchs, prosperity is seen as a sign of God's blessing. It is the fruit of righteousness (Prov 21:21; Ps 112) and of trusting in God (Prov 28:25). Humility and fear of God lead to wealth, honour and life (Prov 22:4). Down-to-earth advice is offered in the reminder that laziness leads to poverty (Prov 10:4) while hard work has the opposite effect (Prov 28:19–20). Wisdom itself and sound teaching are also linked to wealth (Prov 3:2, 13, 14). This was certainly the case with Solomon, seen as the father of Israel's wisdom. When God asked him what he most wanted, he replied, 'Wisdom'. God gave him the wisdom and the silver and gold that a lesser man would have asked for. The prophet Malachi was able to promise the people of his day that if they were faithful in their tithing (ie giving a tenth of their income to God) they would receive great material blessing in response (Mal 3:10).

The wicked prosper too

The books of Psalms and Job, in particular, recognise that taken by itself this 'prosperity teaching' is too shallow. It lacks the depth to relate to real life with all its contradictions. Thus a second theological line is opened up, which seems to be at odds with the first. Hence this statement: 'For I envied the arrogant, when I saw the prosperity of the wicked' (Ps 73:3). This is typical of a refrain that runs through many of the Psalms, based on the observation that in fact many of the righteous do not prosper, while many of the evil and wicked seem to do very well for themselves. So we find the question repeatedly asked, 'Why do the evil prosper?'

The book of Job takes up the issue, in its moving story of a godly man whose entire family, fortune and happiness is wrecked by a string of personal tragedies. While Job's life is in ruins, he sees that the lives of many bad people are going from strength to strength.

> Why do the wicked live on,
> growing old and increasing in power?
> They see their children established around them,
> their offspring before their eyes.
> Their homes are safe and free from fear;
> the rod of God is not upon them.
> Their bulls never fail to breed;
> their cows calve and do not miscarry (Job 21:7–10).

The book of Job never tries to give quick and easy answers to what are some of the most difficult questions in life. It finally destroys any suggestion of a comfortable easy-going prosperity theology.

The prophet Malachi had to deal with a virtual mutiny of God's people, who had been led to believe that if they were faithful to God they would prosper. In effect they turned their religion into justification by works, believing that God was somehow morally bound to bless them. When they saw the evil prospering better than themselves they were ready to give up on God (Mal 3:14–15). This attitude is still very strong today.

We are left here with an open-ended issue, to which the Bible offers no straightforward and dogmatic answer. Each incident is a uniquely individual one before God. The question is left as an open wound in the minds of God's people. This dilemma continues to present itself to every generation, up to and including our own. On the one hand, faithful followers of God offer testimony to how he has blessed them materially, and on the other hand equally faithful followers live in abject poverty, while the godless often prosper in their health, wealth and family fortunes.

Warnings about wealth

Despite its positive attitude to prosperity, Wisdom Literature is also part of the biblical line of thought which warns against the corrupting and enslaving potential of material wealth. The commandment 'Thou shalt not covet' had not just been given as a safeguard of social justice for the community. It also had an individual application, protecting the person's heart against the love of money. Take away this safeguard and the individual is liable to deteriorate into becoming one of the 'fat and heavy', 'greasy and greedy' (Deut 32:15; Jer 5:27).

Material wealth exerts a powerful temptation (Job 36:18), which in the case of Achan was too strong to resist (Josh 7:20). The desire for wealth twists the human mind: 'Whoever loves money never has money enough; whoever loves wealth is never satisfied' (Eccles 5:10). It is not worth it to wear oneself out, just to acquire money (Prov 23:4), for no one can take it with them when they die (Ps 39:6; Prov 11:4).

These warnings against 'money-lust' are essential in any capitalist society, where greed and simple materialism are part of the normal way of life. To imagine that they apply merely to the very rich is naive; they apply to all those who have chance and inclination to acquire and enjoy more than the essentials in life.

The poor are special

As noted above, the Wisdom Literature builds on the idea of 'the poor' being a special group of people, in God's mind's eye, and for whom he has a special loving concern. The book of Job contains one of the truly great and painful descriptions of poverty in Chapter 24. To these hungry folk God provides food and drink (Ps 132:15); he is their refuge (Ps 14:6); he hears and saves the poor man (Ps 34:6); he rescues him from the powerful (Ps 35:10), giving him justice and protection (Ps 82:3). 'He raises the poor from the dust and lifts the needy from the ash heap' (Ps 113:7).

Israel's ideal kingly Messiah will defend the afflicted, save the children of the needy, and crush the oppressor. He will take pity on the weak and hear their cry (Ps 72). He will deprive the powerful of their rights and help the poor to forget their poverty (Prov 31:4–9).

Throughout the book of Proverbs there is a liberal sprinkling of verses, calling for special care, compassion and charity to be shown to the needy (Prov 14:21; 21:13; 22:9). They are to be befriended (Prov 14:20) and accepted equally as created by God (Prov 22:2). To treat them badly is to treat God badly (Prov 14:31; 19:17).

Many of these Wisdom teachings have echoes elsewhere in the Old Testament, and find greater development and enrichment in the New Testament.

In Summary

The major Old Testament theme of wealth and poverty is represented by the events, laws and teachings surrounding the covenant community. These traditions are renewed and upheld by the prophets and passed on to the New Testament church. They represent equality, freedom and true justice for all; protection and special provision for the most vulnerable; a fair distribution of national wealth.

In addition, a secondary theme focuses more on the individual's private life and attitudes. This highlights the positive aspects of prosperity, while it also realises that there are potential problems with it. Pre-dating Timothy's warnings on the love of money, it recognises the awesome power of the covetous tendency in humanity.

Throughout the Old Testament there develops the notion that the poor hold a special eternal place in the affections and intentions of God.

Note

1. Gustavo Gutierrez, *We Drink from Our Own Wells* (SCM: London, 1984).

CHAPTER FIVE

THE NEW TESTAMENT

For the remainder of biblical history, from the Exile through to the New Testament period, Israel was always a small and insignificant part of someone else's empire, Babylonian, Persian, Greek and finally Roman (apart from a brief period of national independence before the time of Jesus).

This meant paying taxes to foreign rulers, importing alien customs and losing control of their own affairs. Throughout this period the wealthy increasingly aligned themselves with the foreign overlord, thus protecting and even increasing their wealth. In contrast, the poor became poorer: many lost what land they had and became casual labourers; destitution and beggary increased. Violence, banditry and insurrection thrived in such conditions, while the pious often retreated behind monastic walls. These background conditions are seen clearly in the events and parables of Jesus and in those later writings which are rooted in Israel, ie the letter of James and the early chapters of Acts. Other New Testament writings take us into other areas of the empire and often have local conditions against which they have to be understood.

The principal sources for New Testament teaching on wealth and poverty are the Gospels, in particular the Gospels of Matthew and Luke. In each case the writers or compilers of the Gospels have used their material to bring out a different emphasis. Matthew tends to think of the poor in a spiritual context, following the Old Testament tradition of the poor as the humble and lowly, while the poor in Luke are generally those suffering material poverty. Both are well aware of the dangers of riches, but Luke is particularly sharp and definite on the issue. These differing emphases are illustrated in the Beatitudes. Matthew records Jesus as saying 'Blessed are the poor in spirit', and Luke has Jesus saying 'Blessed are the poor' balanced by his powerful 'Woe to the rich'. This is not to say, however, that Matthew 'spiritualises' the poor (as many do today); he has much to say about the pain of material poverty and the power of prosperity. Similarly Luke does not think exclusively of the material; he is very aware of the spiritual dimension in the lives of rich and poor alike.

Much Old Testament teaching is concerned with organising the corporate side of life, laying down laws, ordering community, establishing political and social justice. In contrast the New Testament focuses on the individual: on the struggle in the individual's life to put God first before one's own worldly desires; on the individual's own morality, generosity and awareness of others. The corporate and political viewpoint is certainly not ignored, but it is seen as developing out of the individual's conversion, life of obedience and joining with other individuals to form communities of the 'God-centred'. Jesus brought the kingdom of God—with its gift of eternal life, healing powers, infusion of the Holy Spirit, and new radical 'love values'—to the individual's life, and sought through the individual to transform society and the world.

The New Testament can in one sense be thought of as the 'Jesus Testament'. Its story is of his coming, his teaching and the impact he had on other people's lives. Its teaching and insights concerning wealth and poverty are woven around and emerge out of the 'Jesus event'. Following on from this we can try to follow and understand these teachings by arranging them into three sections: the coming of Jesus, the teaching of Jesus, and the community of Jesus.

In each of these sections the primary source of information consists of the Gospels themselves. However, the later New Testament writings have a vital contribution to make and can still be considered as the outworking of the Jesus Event.

The coming of Jesus

Incarnation into poverty

The coming of Jesus represents the Creator of the universe actually bursting in to a small part of his creation. Yet this bursting-in was done not with splendour, bright lights and powerful acclamations but quietly, humbly and in a lowly fashion. 'He was in the world and though the world was made through him the world did not recognise him' (Jn 1:11). Conrad Boerma describes it as a birth into poverty: 'Jesus is the embodiment of the poor man. He does not attempt to disown this image. He does not look for ways of being reconciled with the state. Ambition and greed are alien to him.'[1]

If Jesus had been born as the world's richest king it would still have been a great lowering of himself. In fact he was born as a child of the poor. The breathtaking irony of the event is well illustrated by the visit of the Magi, coming automatically to the court of King Herod, to greet the new-born king.

Far from being born in a palace, the new-born King was not even born in a house. He was a homeless one, soon to be a refugee with the descent into Egypt, son of a young girl from 'up north', and welcomed at his birth by poor shepherds. When he was presented in the Temple his parents could not afford the standard offering so they offered two pigeons, a special 'poor persons' rate. The familiar details of the Christmas stories all make the point that Jesus came among the poor and was one of them. In a world which loves to build fences between the 'haves' and the 'have-nots' he was born, not in a central no-man's-land, but on one particular side of the fence.

Throughout his life he continued to live as a poor man. He had few possessions and no roots in land or home-ownership (Lk 9:58). However, he was no thin-faced ascetic; he wore an expensive seamless robe, attended rich houses and parties, and accepted a costly gift of adoration (Mt 26:7). Like all poor people he was ultimately a servant, his only piece of independent wealth was his own life, and even this he gave away (Mk 10:45).

This theme of poverty is essential to our understanding of the incarnation, ie the coming of God in human form. Certainly Paul fully understood it, and taught it to others in Philippians 2:6–8 and in 2 Corinthians 8:9: 'For you know the grace of our Lord Jesus Christ, that though he was rich, yet for your sakes he became poor, so that you through his poverty might become rich.'

Paul himself entered into his own incarnation into poverty in his following of Jesus (2 Cor 6:10).

Signs of the kingdom

Before Jesus was even born, Mary was given prophetic insight into the whole shape and mission of the life of Jesus her son:

> He has scattered those who are proud in their inmost thoughts. He has brought down rulers from their thrones but has lifted up the humble. He has filled the hungry with good things but has sent the rich away empty (Lk 1:51–53).

In his poverty Jesus was able to fulfil the vision of the suffering servant spoken of by Isaiah, and to bring in the kingdom of God. His day of public emergence came at the synagogue in Nazareth (Lk 4:14–21). Reading from the book of Isaiah he proclaimed that the kingdom of God had come, and that his words and works of eternal life, healing and freedom were the signs of its coming. One of these 'kingdom signs' was the preaching of the gospel to the poor. These were the downcast, the deprived, the broken, habitually despised by the wealthy yet specially treasured by God. God's special love for them had been repeatedly manifested through the Old Testament law codes, Psalms and prophecies and was openly demonstrated in Jesus. In proclaiming the 'year of the Lord's favour' he was bringing into history the year of jubilee, a year for cancelling all debts, for bringing the rich down to earth and lifting the poor up off their knees (Lev 25). Hundreds of years previously, God had instituted the year of jubilee as a national institution, yet the rich and powerful had never allowed it to happen; but now Jesus was making it happen.

Again in Matthew we see Jesus as the servant bringing in the kingdom, with justice (12:18), with cancelling of debt (18:23), by fair distribution of wealth (20:1).

When the Baptist's disciples came to ask Jesus if he really was the true kingdom Messiah, he pointed to the signs that were becoming real through his ministry: 'The blind receive sight, the lame walk, those who have leprosy are cured, the dead are raised and the good news is preached to the poor' (Lk 7:22).

The kingdom comes into open conflict with the world of the wealthy and acts against the unfairness of the kingdom of this world. This clash of the kingdoms is seen violently in the cleansing of the Temple. Exploitation of the religious zeal of the devout and manipulation and cheating of the poor were actually accepted and respectable practices. To Jesus, however, they represent the enemy; they are driven out and the Temple is reclaimed for God. The same conflict is seen in a pagan context in Acts 19:23–41. The silversmiths of Ephesus were making money out of the people's misguided paganism. Paul's evangelism was not just a challenge to individuals to follow Christ, it was also a declaration of Holy War against a sinful and worldly system.

As a poor man's Messiah, as the bringer of the kingdom to the poor and the sick, Jesus was expressing and enacting the very special love of God for the underdog. In this way he was fulfilling, but also taking to new depths God's 'underdog' love, which had previously been promised through the teaching of the Old Testament.

The teaching of Jesus

Jesus' ministry consisted in the main of healing, exorcisms, miracles and teachings all woven around the reality of the kingdom of God. He taught that a person enters into the kingdom, and that the kingdom enters into a person (in effect two different perspectives in the one experience) through repentance, forgiveness and baptism, and that the person's subsequent kingdom life is made real through his continuing obedience to the will of God, the king.

A vital aspect of this process of conversion and kingdom living is a person's attitude towards money and possessions, rich and poor people, equality and social justice, and the needs of the wider community. In fact Jesus considered this whole area to be so important that he spoke more about it than about any other subject apart from the kingdom itself. For most of us today who spend little time thinking about this, or listening to sermons about such issues, it often comes as quite a shock to realise that there are more references to money than there are to heaven, on the lips of Jesus.

Jesus's teaching is essentially concerned with the struggle between two rival kingdoms, one offering earthly pleasure, the other eternal life. Every person has to reach an individual choice as to which kingdom they will serve. This choice also brings with it certain principles, moral values and lifelong commitments. These should dictate not only the individual (ie personal) life of the 'Jesus person' but also his community (ie political) life.

Two masters

'No servant can serve two masters. Either he will hate the one and love the other, or he will be devoted to the one and despise the other. You cannot serve both God and money' (Lk 16:13).

Jesus's evangelism here is like a spiritual tug of war. He is not just asking for a prayer of commitment, nor even for people to join their local church. He is calling on men and women to enter the kingdom of God. Yet he realises that there is also at work an opposing dark presence calling them to remain in the kingdom of this world. This enemy he here identified with 'Mammon', the alluring power of money, possessions and worldly security. The worldliness wants to master humankind, ie it wants to be God.

We are accustomed to thinking of money as a neutral thing, which can be good or bad depending on the user; yet Jesus here goes beyond this, arguing that money actually has a power of its own and wants to exert its mastery over human weakness. Rather than money being a servant of man, there is a great danger of the reverse, that man ends up serving money. Thus in the parable of the sower, Jesus warns of the power of money to deceive and choke to death the new believer (Mt 13:22), and to a man who was over-interested in his inheritance he declared 'Watch out, be on your guard against all kind of greed' (Lk 12:15). Richard Foster argues for this understanding of rival mastership:

> When Jesus uses the Aramaic term Mammon to refer to wealth, he is giving it a personal and spiritual character. He is personifying Mammon as a rival God. In saying this, Jesus is making it unmistakably clear that money is not some impersonal medium of exchange. Money is not something that is morally neutral, a resource to be used in good or bad ways depending solely on our attitude towards it. Mammon is a power that seeks to dominate us.[2]

So in response to Jesus's kingdom-based evangelistic challenge the individual has to choose between God and worldly pleasure and comfort. 'If anyone would come after me, he must deny himself... What good is it for a man to gain the whole world, and yet lose or forfeit his very self?' (Lk 9:23–25).

Two treasures

The choice between the two kingdoms, each with their own master, is developed in Jesus's reference to the two different types of treasure:

> Do not store up for yourselves treasures on earth, where moth and rust destroy, and where thieves break in and steal. But store up for yourselves treasures in heaven, where moth and rust do not destroy, and where thieves do not break in and steal. For where your treasure is, there your heart will be also (Mt 6:19–21).

Treasure here means the things we really desire, for which we plan and prepare and to which we devote time and energy. It is the whole purpose and goal of our life, that which we would most like to pass on to our children or friends. This idea of the two treasures recurs later in the New Testament: earthly treasure becomes corroded and moth-eaten (Jas 5:2–3), while heavenly treasure is found only in Christ (Col 2:3) and is given by him to the faithful (2 Cor 4:7; Heb 11:26).

Luke's Gospel shows us three characters, all serving the mastership of money, all trying to accumulate earthly treasure.

The Rich Fool lives a fool's life serving the God of this world, and dies a fool's death, never having known the God of life (Lk 12:14–20).

The Rich Man is dressed in purple and fine linen; he walks past Lazarus, a poor beggar, and never acknowledges his presence. He ignores the teaching of Moses and the prophets, and when he dies he spends eternity in hell (Lk 16:19–31).

The Rich Young Ruler came looking to Jesus for eternal life, but for him this would mean giving up his wealth. This he could not do, because in effect his wealth was not his servant but his master. He went away from Jesus rich but unhappy.

In teaching the potential evil and destructive effects of money Jesus was continuing a tradition begun by the Old Testament commandment 'Thou shalt not Covet'. This tradition runs through the Psalms, prophets and Wisdom Literature of the late Old Testament, and extends beyond the Gospels:

> People who want to get rich fall into temptation and a trap and into many foolish and harmful desires that plunge men into ruin and destruction. For the love of money is a root of all kinds of evil. Some people, eager for money, have wandered from the faith (1 Tim 6:9–10).

James follows this up with warnings against greed and covetousness, and of how desire for pleasure leads to bitterness and violence (Jas 4:1–3). It seems that money almost always brings out the worst in people, and, even in the church, people handling it should be extra careful to avoid intrigue and scandal (2 Cor 8:2–21).

Two daily breads

For those who are seeking the kingdom of God and his righteous living first and foremost in life, there is no longer any pressure to worry about worldly security. The father who clothes and provides for birds, animals and all the natural world will feed and clothe them (Mt 6:25–34). This encouragement to simple trust in God's provision is again expressed in the prayerful petition for 'daily bread'. The picture is not of a mean rationing God who provides the minimum for a bare material existence here on earth, but rather of a generous God who loves to give good gifts both spiritual and material to his children (Lk 11:5–13). This is the God who maintained the Jews in the wilderness not on a frugal amount, but on more than they were able to gather in and eat (Jn 6:58). When Jesus himself gave daily bread at the feeding of the five thousand, he gave so much that there were twelve basketfuls left over.

Judgement and riches

Perhaps the most difficult aspect of Jesus's teaching for us to accept and apply to our own lives is the close connection he establishes between riches and judgement. It is easier for a camel to get through the eye of a needle than for a rich man to get through the entrance to heaven (Lk 18:25). The disciples were clearly shocked by this saying, as we are today. In the Beatitudes of Matthew 5 and Luke 6 Jesus promises blessedness, feeding and heaven to the poor who have received so little in this world. As for the rich, they have had all their blessings in the 'here and now', and should dread the future.

> But woe to you who are rich,
> for you have already received your comfort.
> Woe to you who are well fed now,
> for you will go hungry.
> Woe to you who laugh now,
> for you will mourn and weep (Lk 6:24, 25).

Yet Jesus did not automatically dispatch all the rich to hell. Joseph of Aramathea was a follower of Jesus but he was also a rich man (Mt 27:57), and Nicodemus probably fell into the same category. There were certain women who used their wealth to support Jesus and the disciples. Zacchaeus gave half of his fortune away, but the half he kept would certainly have maintained him in a comfortable lifestyle.

Jesus seems to have been more concerned about the twisted and distorted values and personalities that usually go with wealth than with the money itself. The danger in saying this is that everyone breathes a sigh of relief, feeling that their attitude and personality is acceptable, so they can expect to hang on to their creature comforts and still go to heaven. It should be remembered from the story of the rich young ruler that the attitude Jesus was looking for was an active willingness to give up worldly wealth and to make the will of God the first priority in life. Jesus's words to the rich are hard and have sharp edges; we may want to blunt the edges and lessen the impact, but Jesus never tried to soften them and offer false comfort.

This strand of teaching is extended into the later New Testament. James speaks of the rich who weep and wail because of the misery that is coming upon them (5:1), while the poor are preparing to inherit the kingdom (2:5). Revelation brings the whole idea to a climax. The letters to the churches provide a telling contrast between the church in Smyrna (2:8), based in a hostile city, suffering afflictions and poverty, yet clearly esteemed by God, and the church of Laodicea. This was a comfortable rich church, in a comfortable rich city. Their affluence seems to have led to spiritual apathy, and God is ready to spit them out of his mouth (3:14). Later on in the book as judgement draws close, the powerful, mighty and rich attempt to hide away in caves (6:15). Finally, greed and all the unfair and exploitive systems that it gives birth to are brought down with the great whore of Babylon (Rev 18). Babylon symbolises the kingdom of Mammon which thrives throughout the whole of human history and in every nation, city and community. Covetousness, lust, and desire are the energy system of Babylon; inequality, deprivation and godlessness its fruits. The battle of the kingdoms is finally resolved in victory for the kingdom of God (Rev 18:16–17).

Today, however, financial affluence and an abundance of worldly goods is no longer the prerogative of the rich. A high percentage of Western Christians are now living on good wages, in houses full of creature comforts. (Probably the majority of clergy, who habitually complain about how poorly they are paid, are in this 'easy life' category.) Many of us have a troubled conscience about our lifestyle. Rather than laying down fixed laws, it seems to me that Jesus presents us with a series of hard questions:

Do I really love God more than my house, possessions, car, etc?

Do I go on buying extra 'things' because I have a need for them, or because I have spare cash?

Do I give at least a tenth of my income to church mission?

On top of this tenth, do I share joyfully of my wealth with those around me who are less well off?

Does my wealth mark me and my family out as being 'better off' in the context of my local church and neighbourhood?

If I live in an affluent church and neighbourhood, do I have any real contact with poorer Christians in my town or denomination?

Do I make any contribution to global issues, eg Greenpeace, Amnesty International, Tear Fund?

Love and justice for the poor

Expanding on the rather hard expression 'the poor', Moltmann has this to say:

> The collective term 'the poor' covers the hungry, the unemployed, the sick, the discouraged, and the sad and suffering. The poor are the subjected, oppressed and humiliated people (*ochlos*). The poor are sick, crippled, homeless (Lk 14:21–23). They are the beggars in the streets and on the country roads (Mt 11:2–5). They are the sad (Lk 6:21).[3]

We have already seen how the Magnificat (Lk 1), the 'signs of the kingdom' and the Beatitudes (especially the extended version in Mt 5), all continue the Old Testament tradition of God's special love for the poor. Here God is seen as having a unique compassion and blessing for those who have got so little out of this world. This tradition is brought to life by Jesus's parable of the great banquet (Lk 14:15). Here the invited guests fail to turn up to the great occasion, and so the host sends out fresh invitations, this time to the poor, the crippled, the blind and the lame. There is still room left, so again the invitations go out, to the roads and country lanes (ie to the homeless, the wanderers, the beggars). This parable was offered by Jesus as an illustration of God's great heavenly banquet.

Perhaps the contrast between rich and poor is seen most clearly in the observation made by Jesus concerning people's offerings. He describes the rich making large yet non-costly gifts into the Temple treasury, while the poor widow's gift of two coins was all she had and represented a truly generous and thankful heart (Lk 21:1–4).

While love and justice are often thought to be in conflict, in fact they belong together. God's love for the unloved arouses his sense of justice. Jesus was God's compaigner for justice for all his creatures who are unjustly deprived of their God-given birth-right. This note of justice first sounded in the Magnificat, and was echoed in the teachings of John the Baptist. He called upon those with plenty of clothing and food to share with those who had none; he attacked corrupt taxation, which then (as in so much of history) was unfairly balanced against the poor; and he called upon the soldiers, men with real power to frighten, not to abuse their position of trust (Lk 3:11–14). In his own time Jesus attacked the Pharisees. Their religion was perfect in its outward show of respectability and orthodoxy, but their ignoring of the needs of the poor and the demands of justice made it empty hypocrisy (Lk 11:41–43; Mt 23:23).

He accepted the legal authority of Rome and of its imposed taxation (Mt 17:24), but he remained adamant that all authority, influence and glory that belonged to God should be rendered to him alone. Furthermore he was not blind to the overbearing presence and injustice of the Roman dictatorships: 'You know that the leaders of the Gentiles lord it over them' (Mt 20—25).

These two qualities of God's love and justice are brought mightily together in the parable of the sheep and goats (Mt 25:31–46). Here, in painful love and in unswerving justice, Jesus declares that if there must always be injustice, inequality and alienation, then he will always stand with the recipient of such brutality. He will literally become one of the poor, so that when the 'non-poor' help the poor they are helping Jesus, and when they ignore them they are ignoring Jesus. On that day those who have been first throughout their earthly lives will suddenly be last, while those who stood at the back of the queue will suddenly be first (Mt 20:16).

The Old Testament belief in justice and equality worked through the law codes, and was spoken out by the prophets against the social and political structure of the state. In a state where the overwhelming majority of the population, including the aristocracy, the civil servants, the politicians, the army generals and the monarchy all claim to be faithful servants of God, this is a sensible thing to do. The New Testament church, however, was in a completely different situation. It was a microscopic and totally irrelevant part of the political movements of the Roman Empire. As a result there are no clearly marked political messages in it, and who would have taken notice of such messages? However, to argue from this that Jesus and the New Testament writers were not interested in politics and have nothing to say to the political situation is pure escapism. As we have seen, there are vital principles which run through the Gospels. These reappear later in the New Testament; for example: 'At the present time your plenty will supply what they need, so that in turn their plenty will supply what you need. Then there will be equality' (2 Cor 8:14). 'Look! the wages you failed to pay the workmen who mowed your fields are crying out against you. The cries of the harvesters have reached the ears of the Lord Almighty' (Jas 5:4).

Such statements have 'Jesus' written all over them. All Christians know in their heart of hearts that truth, justice, fairness, equality and compassion are hallmarks of Jesus, of God and his kingdom, and that these are supreme human qualities which should apply in all human communities; they apply to family life, inter-church relationships, the workplace and the political life of a city or nation. When we look at the Jesus community we will see attempts to ground these principles in real human living.

Generous giving

In an unjust world God's gift of prosperity for all will always be abused. One section of the community will always take more than its fair share. This is the experience of virtually every human society that has progressed beyond the initial nomadic, gathering state. This was Israel's experience throughout the Old Testament, and the prophetic analysis of that history was that one man's affluence represents ten men's poverty. Jim Wallis has beautifully captured this injustice and our distorted perception of it: 'The question to be asked is not what we should give to the poor but when we will stop taking from the poor. The poor are not our problem; we are their problem.'[4]

Jesus's oft-quoted statement about the prevalence of the poor should be read against this historical and spiritual background. 'The poor you will always have with you' (Mt 26:11) is not a resigned acceptance of the inevitability of poverty, but is rather a realistic, painful and prophetic appraisal of human nature.

Charity is a poor second best for justice (especially for those having to depend on it). In a world where justice and equality are in such short supply there has to be deep and generous giving. So Jesus calls on the Pharisees, his own disciples and all his would-be devout listeners to give to the poor (Lk 11:41).

Even if it means selling one's own possessions (Lk 12:33), such free and generous giving should be an expression of what a person has received from God's free and generous gift of life (Mt 10:8). Such giving should be offered privately where there is no human audience to offer congratulations (Mt 6:2). It is not enough, however, to give to the poor and 'keep them at a distance'. Far more challenging is Jesus's provocative suggestion that people should open their doors to offer them hospitality and send out party invitations (Lk 14:13–14). The normal posture of charity is patronising; the giver looks down from his height to the grateful and lowly recipient. Jesus replaces this with a posture of neighbourliness. Anyone who is broken down and attacked by life is my neighbour. He is an equal, but he needs my neighbouring love, at the particular point of his hardship. This radical concept of 'neighbouring responsibility' as opposed to 'patronising charity' is the message of the parable of the good Samaritan. In the past this story has been hijacked by left-wing politicans as a defence of Socialism; today it is in danger of being hijacked by the right, arguing that the fact that the Samaritan actually had money in his pocket is a defence of private enterprise. Neither interpretation is acceptable; the essential thrust of Jesus's message is pure and unmistakable.

The New Testament gives two great examples of such giving. One is Zacchaeus who, when confronted by Jesus, realises that his wealth is wrong and gives half to the poor (Lk 19). While many of us will know of greater examples of individual giving, few will know of many such examples. Furthermore, one must realise the incredible turnaround this represented for a money-grabbing tyrant. The second example is the collection taken up by the Christians of the New Testament churches for those suffering starvation in Jerusalem. Many of the givers here were themselves poverty-stricken, especially the Macedonians (2 Cor 8:2). Perhaps it was from these that Paul himself learned the liberating joy of giving, and the divine response 'for God loves a cheerful giver' (2 Cor 9:7).

He counselled the Corinthians to work hard at keeping up to their commitment to give (2 Cor 8:11) and to work out carefully how much they could and would give (2 Cor 9:7). Such giving should not be seen as drudgery (2 Cor 9:5) but as a privilege, an expression of love towards God (2 Cor 8:4, 8). This commitment to giving is particularly laid at the door of the more wealthy members of a congregation (1 Tim 6:17–19).

This type of giving is a stop-gap in a sinful, cruel world. Nevertheless, it is still vital and necessary and should not be derided, for, when offered in the right spirit, it actually becomes part of the outworking love of God for the poor and lowly.

The community of Jesus

Jesus's entrance into the world had a huge impact that was both wide and deep: wide, in that many thousands heard or saw something of him as he moved round the country teaching, healing, feeding and being totally involved with people; deep, in that a minority of these thousands were hugely disturbed by him. For some, this disturbance led to fear and hatred, but for others it developed positively into devotion. They followed him spiritually, in their hearts, and to some extent physically, on the road. They accepted his teachings and committed themselves to repentance, faith and obedience. They were the beginnings of the Jesus community.

The early stages

This small group of followers gradually evolved from a rather mixed bag of personalities, into a tightly-knit community. In the days of Jesus' ministry it included fishermen, a tax collector, a political revolutionary, a converted prostitute, orthodox Jews and heavy party-goers. These were people who would normally have been enemies, but who were gradually forced (perhaps unwillingly) into becoming brothers. The group contained some rich and influential people: Joseph of Arimathea, a rich man; Nicodemus, a member of the Jewish ruling council; Joanna, the wife of Chuza, the manager of Herod's household. It seems as though Jesus and the twelve formed an inner core, depending on the financial support of a section of women members (Lk 8:1–3).

While some of these followers probably remained in their normal home and life routine, others left everything behind— work, friends and family—and literally followed him (Lk 18:28). This group of immediate followers was sent out by Jesus with no bag, no bread, no money, no extra tunic, ie without any of the normal sources of support and material security; in other words they were learning to depend on God alone for their earthly needs (Lk 9:3). A secondary and larger group of seventy-two was sent out to the towns and villages with similar instructions, as the pattern of living by faith was established.

As this loose grouping of people came closer together, personalities and egos began to jostle for influence and leadership. This is a normal and inevitable human process and happens in all groups of people. In this group, however, Jesus reversed the normal power-play of human nature:

> You know that those who are regarded as rulers of the Gentiles lord it over them, and their high officials exercise authority over them. Not so with you. Instead, whoever wants to become great among you must be your servant, and whoever wants to be first must be slave of all (Mk 10:42–44).

Thus Jesus takes the normal hierarchy of a pyramid and turns it upside down, replacing leadership based on power, wealth and privilege, with that based on humility and vocation.

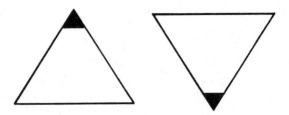

This radical 'group-life' principle was the basis of Jesus's own leadership, and was enacted at the Last Supper with the washing of the disciples' feet.

The emerging church

These pioneer followers travelled through the crucifixion, Resurrection and Ascension with Jesus and with each other. This shared experience must have had an incalculable effect, not only on them as individuals, but on them as a group. This shared experience was enriched, enlivened and empowered by their receiving of the Pentecostal Spirit. Thus sharing their memories of Jesus and the fire of the Spirit they were welded together into the Jesus community, which represented God taking the least valued of human society, the people at the bottom of the pile, and turning them into new types of human beings. This community saw itself as the servant of the world and fulfilled three vital roles in its servanthood.

First, it posed a revolutionary challenge to the class-based structure of the human hierarchy. The Greek-Roman world of the New Testament was extremely class-conscious. Money, power, influence and breeding were all vital and much-valued parts of a person's sense of worth and dignity. (English culture bears great similarities to it.) Paul's description of the make-up of the church shows that the Jesus community was operating on revolutionary principles:

> Not many of you were wise by human standards; not many were influential; not many were of noble birth. But God chose the foolish things of the world to shame the wise; God chose the weak things of the world to shame the strong. He chose the lowly things of this world and the despised things—and the things that are not—to nullify the things that are (1 Cor 1:26-28).

When the church begins to nullify the things of this world, then it is being truly revolutionary. Today we are massively conservative and traditionalist; we accept the status quo of society and even play a big part in protecting and supporting it; yet all the time we are supposed to be signalling its break-up.

Secondly, the Jesus community provided a healing model for broken human society. The inner relationships of the Christian community are characteristically described by the word *philadelphia*—brotherhood, fraternity. Thirty times in Acts and 130 times in Paul's writing, the word is used to convey the sense of the very special bonding ties that the first Christians enjoyed. Whether Jews or Greeks, slave or free... all were given the one

Spirit' (1 Cor 12:13). Against the background of society's great inequalities Paul establishes the concept of equality (1 Cor 8:13). Equality is not meant as a vain Utopian ideal but as a hard realistic fact, flowing out of Christian brotherhood. Here the poor, be they the hungry victims of famine (Acts 11:27) or the weak and vulnerable, eg widows (1 Tim 5:3–16), would receive special help and attention from the non-poor. Conrad Boerma argues that it was actually this quality of Christian community life that was the main factor leading to the spread of Christianity.

> There is historical evidence to show that the attraction of the first community did not lie in its missionary campaigns (there is virtually no call to evangelise in any of the epistles), but in its way of life. Their very real brotherhood made Christ's community particularly attractive to a world which was so disrupted by social conflicts. If people could live like this, their God must be very special.[5]

Of course, the delicate balance of brotherhood and equality was easily threatened by the insensitive intrusion of wealth. The better-off members of the church in Corinth could be crudely ostentatious and selfish with their money and expensive food and drink (1 Cor 11:22), while those of the Jerusalem church were clearly 'puffed up' and uncaring for the poor (Jas 1:9–11). When rich new converts or members appeared in their fine clothes alongside poorer newcomers there was a danger of favouritism, so James is keen to remind everyone of their proper place within the Jesus community (Jas 2:1–4).

The church was a community based on sharing: 'All the believers were together and had everything in common. Selling their possessions and goods they gave to anyone in need' (Acts 22:44). 'All the believers were one in heart and mind. No one claimed that any of his possessions were his own, but they shared everything they had (Acts 4:32).

Yet this was not a compulsory, legalistic sharing, as was then practised and is still practised by many religious groups. It was a sharing based on freedom. Ananias and Sapphira were not forced to share their wealth with the group; they were free to keep their possessions. In effect they wanted the best of both worlds and tried to cover the joint with deceit (Acts 6:1–10). There were certain rich individuals in the early church who continued to hold on to their wealth and use it, often for the good of others (Rom 16:23; Acts 18:8; 1 Cor 16:15–17).

Hundreds of years later a class-bound Europe suffering poverty and brutality would cry out for liberty, fraternity and equality with revolutionary fervour. The Jesus community was not a revolutionary group, but it was a revolutionary concept in human living. It demonstrated these great ideals and more, and it established a model and a pattern for others to follow.

Thirdly, it gave life to the dying world. The earliest Christian community recognised men and women as complete human beings. As a direct continuation of Jesus's special love and mission to the poor and needy, they offered food and money where it was most needed. In Jerusalem a daily distribution of food to widows was organised (Acts 6:1), while in Joppa one of the disciples called Dorcas was well known for helping the poor. They also continued Jesus' healing ministry, seeing illness both physical and spiritual as a real cause of poverty.

Alongside this concern for people's social needs, there was a very powerful movement committed to their spiritual needs. The first Christians were not evangelistic soul hunters, excluding all other aspects of humanity's needs and of God's love (unlike many evangelical churches today), but they were nevertheless very powerfully evangelistic (unlike the overwhelming majority of churches today). Three thousand people were converted at the preaching of the first Christian evangelistic sermon (Acts 2); Peter and John were not able to give the beggar either food or money, but they were able and willing to give him the new life of worldwide evangelistic strategy.

Unlike most of us today they saw the full extent of men's poverty as being social and spiritual, and they set out to feed it.

Summary: The Irrelevant Church and the Bible

1. Thinking about the issues of wealth and poverty, about justice and exploitation, about God's church and God's world, it is possible to discern various principles which are traced through the development of biblical thought. These principles have been summarised at various points through this survey of Bible teaching, but very briefly they can be stated again.

   - All wealth is given by God.
   - There is sufficient for everyone's need.
   - All who can should work hard and honestly.
   - A rich/poor divide with all the inevitable deprivation and exploitation that it brings is seen as evil, and is consistently attacked throughout the prophetic tradition.
   - God has a special love for the poor.
   - Jesus was God's incarnation into poverty.
   - Money is seen virtually as an alternative to Jesus and his kingdom.
   - Jesus established the church as a sharing, caring and converting community.

2. Having discerned and outlined these principles we then have to decide what we will do with them, or what we will allow them to do with us. Do we water them down, ignore them, spiritualise them, obey them, or perhaps just continue living uncomfortably with them? Do we just apply them to our own individual life or do we try to apply them to the life of our church, local community and society? Do we allow them to penetrate our life-style, our pocket, our politics and our religion?

3. These are radical principles. They could be held and retained by a small handful, who would then enjoy a sort of individualistic radicalism. Alternatively they can be passed on, preached about, discussed and written about. Exhibitions,

marches, drama and music could all be generated, and action could be based on them. In this way, radical principles could produce radical people who would then change the church into a radical movement. In this way the church could discover a new relevance.

At the end of the day it is all about commitment. God is not a neutral observer, but a committed activist. At the incarnation Jesus 'signed up' to play for the under-privileged. This is not surprising, for they had always been his Father's favourite team.

Notes

1. Conrad Boerma, *Rich Man, Poor Man* (SCM: London, 1979).
2. Richard Foster, *Money, Sex and Power* (Hodder & Stoughton: London, 1987).
3. Jurgen Moltmann, *The Way of Jesus Christ* (SCM: London, 1990).
4. Jim Wallis, *The Call to Conversion* (Lion Publishing: Tring, 1986).
5. Conrad Boerma, *op cit*.

Part III

*The Irrelevant Church
and the World*

CHAPTER SIX

THE TASK FACING THE CHURCH TODAY

The two nations of modern Britain

The Industrial Revolution has been and gone. The mills and factories, their machinery and workers having been extracted, stand empty now, like toothless skulls. Many of them have disappeared altogether, burnt out by arsonists or laid low by developers. They have been replaced by DIY stores, sprawling car parks or just left as huge holes in the townscape. The forest of mill chimneys which once supported the low grey cloud cover, like pillars in a cathedral, have been brought to their knees. The long rows of terraced houses which had wrapped themselves around the contours of the city hills have been rolled up and discarded like worn-out strips of stair carpet. Some still remain though, cleaned up on the outside, and done up on the inside to create a nineties-style Coronation Street.

Some things, however, never change: the rich are still rich. They've moved a bit farther out of town, they've replaced their horse and carriage with a Ford Granada or BMW, and they've installed expensive burglar alarms to protect their expensive lives. The poor are still with us too, just as Jesus said they always would be: grey soggy bodies, wearing summer clothes in the depths of winter, buying day-old bread and pushing bruised toes into someone else's shoes.

The idea that there are actually two Britains, a rich one and a poor one, is not new. Benjamin Disraeli, who was to become a Conservative Prime Minister, first popularised the idea in 1845, when he published his novel *Sybil*. Egremont, a young aristocrat, is full of enthusiasm as the young Victoria comes to the throne, but the young man he is talking to speaks of the two nations she will reign over:

> 'Yes,' resumed the younger stranger after a moment's interval. 'Two nations; between whom there is no intercourse and no sympathy, who are as ignorant of each other's habits, thoughts, and feelings, as if they were dwellers in different zones, or inhabitants of different planets; who are formed by a different breeding, are fed by a different food, are ordered by different manners, and are not governed by the same laws.'
> 'You speak of—' said Egremont, hesitatingly.
> 'THE RICH AND THE POOR.'

Disraeli was not the only Victorian writer to be shocked by the widening rich/poor divide. Elizabeth Gaskell in her novel *North and South* has her heroine Margaret forced into moving from Hampshire to Manchester. In her new northern habitat she makes this observation:

> I see men here going about in the streets who look ground down by some pinching sorrow or care—who are not only sufferers but haters. Now, in the South we have our poor, but there is not that terrible expression in their countenances of a sullen sense of injustice which I see here.

The 'two nations' picture, however, is even older than Disraeli. The Romans during their occupation of England and Wales drew a line across the country from the Wash to the Severn Valley, calling everything to the north of this *Britannia Inferior* and everything to the south *Britannia Superior*. That line basically still holds good today. John Atherton's book *Faith in the Nation* refers to a prosperity league table developed by Newcastle University.[1] This shows that of the fifty most prosperous towns and cities, forty are to be found in the south, the exceptions being such northern towns as Kendal and Harrogate. At the other end of the table, forty out of the bottom fifty places are occupied by the North.

The Thatcherite revolution and the enterprise culture have been prosperous days for Britain certainly, but for which Britain? During the mid 1980s the top one-fifth of the population saw their share of the country's overall wealth increase from 46.6% to over 48.6%, while the bottom two-fifths saw theirs drop from 8.7% to 6.4%. Those on good earnings see their wages and fringe benefits go up and their tax come down, but those receiving state benefits, at best stand still and in fact usually lose ground.

A tale of two cities

The national picture, however, is not just a simple north–south divide, for there are pockets of real poverty in the south and equally real pockets of wealth in the north. Even a northern post-industrial city like Bradford can be divided into two.

In the first Bradford, people are coming out of work, driving home in a new, or nearly new car, and parking outside their semi-detached or even detached house. Inside, the kids are wearing high-tech trainers and tracksuits or designer jeans and 'top of the pops' tops. The house is full of the latest gadgetry, microwave for mum, 'Black and Decker' for Dad, computers for their kids. Holidays and luxuries that were once a special treat for their parents, are now taken for granted, part of the wallpaper of life. After tea they will go and fill their supermarket trolley to overflowing with bright colours, delicious tastes and large helpings.

While the inhabitants of the first Bradford have never had it so good, those of the second Bradford have just never had it, or not for a long time, anyway. For them the bursting potentialities and promises of life are something they watch other people enjoying on daytime TV. Their clothing, their homes, their diet, their health, their view from the window are all second best. Their happiness has dried up like puddles in the road, their future and their children's future has rusted over before it has even come out of the wrappers. These citizens of the poor man's Bradford will die sooner, smile less and simply spend much of their time shuffling through life.

The picture of two Bradfords is not just based on sentimental images, but on hard statistics.[2] The following table compares two groups of Anglican parishes: not only are they both in the same city, they are actually in the same deanery, but in one sense they are worlds apart.

	Bradford Moor & Bowling Wards	Bolton & Idle Wards
	St Margaret's, Thornbury	St James, Bradford Road
	St Clement's, Bradford Road	St Cuthbert's, Wrose
	St Mary's, Laisterdyke	Holy Trinity, Idle
General Socio-economic Classification	Disadvantaged	Average— Advantaged
Serious overcrowding in housing	4–10%	0.35%
No inside bath or toilet	4%	1%
Homes without a car	over 60%	42%
Unemployment	25%	10%
Crimes reported per household	30%	20%
Free school meals	45%–65%	under 30%
High priority cases of homelessness	44.5 per ward	9.5 per ward
Non-priority cases of homelessness	77 per ward	30 per ward
Dysentery outbreaks in 1984	92 cases	35 cases

Hepatitis cases 1980–83	52	41
Tuberculosis 1975–84	8 per 1000 pop.	1.4 per 1000 pop.
Infant deaths	15 per 1000 pop.	10 per 1000 pop.

The city of Bradford is rather like an uneven chessboard, where about two thirds of all the squares are white areas of prosperity. In among these however are the black squares, the poverty zones, concentrated in the old inner-city area and in the post-war council estates, built to replace the demolished slums.

Willy Russell's musical *Blood Brothers* is a moving and powerful story of two brothers born into poverty after the war. One brother is adopted into the affluence of the first Britain, while the other remains firmly in the second Britain, brought up first in the slums of Liverpool and then moving to a new outer-city housing estate. The gap in terms of quality of life and aspiration between the two is enormous: though they are in effect brothers, their brotherhood is torn in two and all ends in tragic conflict. *Blood Brothers* is a parable, full of truth and reality, about our society.

A tale of two churches

The 'two nations' theory does not just apply to social and economic conditions. Even more shockingly it applies to the churches of all denominations. The one force or movement in society which is supposed to follow its Lord's commitment to the poor and needy, has in effect become a bourgeois institution. Jesus came and actually lived among the poor, but his twentieth-century followers prefer the semis of suburbia. Jesus was the God of the Incarnation, he actually became 'one of us', but today's Christians have opted for incarnation with a nicely trimmed lawn back and front. The kingdom was heralded by the Good News being preached to the poor, but in our churches it is preached to the middle class.

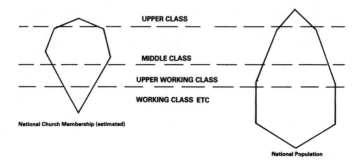

UPPER CLASS

MIDDLE CLASS

UPPER WORKING CLASS

WORKING CLASS ETC

National Church Membership (estimated)

National Population

The church has made a massive retreat in the old inner-city areas. Those churches that do remain, and those that have been planted afresh in the outer-city council estates are often hanging on by their fingertips. Many of Bradford's old town churches and chapels are now long gone, demolished altogether or put to new use selling carpets, furniture and curry suppers. This is not to criticise individual congregations, but merely to state the obvious, that churches and members of all denominations have displayed a consistent determination to move 'up-market'. The Church of England has led the way in despising the culture, language and lifestyle of the working people. In the name of high standards, quality and aesthetics we have produced liturgy, music, visual effects, sermons, etc which are boring, difficult to understand and totally alien to the working classes. These trends have been clear to us now for over a hundred years, yet still the church is incapable of doing much about it.

The result is that a person brought up in a middle-class suburb has a statistically much higher chance of conversion than some-one born on a council estate. Should both characters suddenly decide to go along to their local church on a Sunday morning, the one has a much higher chance of discovering a reasonably pleas-ant building, containing quite a lot of people, many of whom may be young and bright. He or she is more likely to hear a higher calibre of clergyman leading the worship and preaching sermons in a style and vocabulary they can feel part of; the music they hear will probably be better performed and may well involve the use of various instruments. The net result is that a far higher percentage of middle-class people find their way into church and into God, than do working-class people. Bradford, like all other industrial cities in Britain, has a first and a second-class church.

The Evangelical Charismatic wing of the church, which is the most dynamic at the moment, is probably worse than the other traditions in its inbuilt class structure. Many of its best ordinands, clergy and gifted lay people are being sucked into the first-class carriages of the church. Having recently spent three months in one of the country's leading Evangelical theological colleges I am dismayed to see that little has changed since my own time of training. The overwhelming number of ordinands are still from a middle-class, professional or academic background. Local working-class people who feel called to the ministry have to survive an ecclesiastical commando course filled with obstacles that offer little challenge to the middle-class candidate.

Praise God that this is not the total picture. There are exceptions to all these general trends. In Bradford today there are various churches in inner-city areas and outer-city housing estates which are seeing renewal, effective evangelism and penetrating social-gospel missions all going on together. These are however a minority and the general trends remain to govern the majority.

A tale of two rainbows

After the flood, God gave Noah and his descendants a rainbow as a pledge of the safety of his and his family's prosperity. The rainbow was full of bright and vivid colours, because the life of Noah and his descendants was planned by God to be full of bright and vivid things, people, places and experiences.

In the industries, architecture, art and leisure and social and welfare facilities of our society there is more than enough to give everyone the fullness of life as promised by the rainbow. Man however has created two nations, two cities, even two churches. The citizens of the first nation continue to enjoy the life of the multi-coloured rainbow, but the rainbow over the second nation, city and church is not brightly coloured but a combination of dull greys, muddy browns, and watery greens. It symbolises the life lived now and the future anticipated of many people. This society torn in two is the world to which the church of Jesus is called to minister.

The church facing the task

In discussing the church's task, we have first to be clear about what we mean by 'the church'. The church is a universal group of people, covering continents, and stretching over the centuries. In this country we can think of it at three different levels. At the national level, the church is a huge, loosely gathered mass of people with a central belief system roughly corresponding to the orthodox Christian creeds. (Thus I am not here speaking of the national church as the established Church of England.) On the second level we see the various major churches or denominations: Anglican, Roman Catholic, Methodist, House Church, etc. These denominations are usually organised into administrative units, be they dioceses, circuits or whatever. Thirdly, and most important of all, there is the local church. The local church can find great encouragement and sense of purpose from being part of the universal and national church, and it expects to gain direct support and guidance from its denomination. At the end of the day, however, the local church stands or falls as a direct result of what its leadership, its membership and its God do together.

The church is a dynamic and purposeful group of people who each acknowledge the headship of Christ. Jesus is head of the church, universal, national, denominational and local (Eph 2:22). He founded it and it is his mission to build it (Mt 16:18). He chooses to build his church in the power of his Spirit operating through his people.

In one sense the church at each level can be viewed as an institution; in another sense the church is a movement, a fire, a mission.

The church as an institution

The Church of England is the ultimate example in this country of the church as an institution, with a huge and clearly demarcated power structure, administering large areas of land, thousands of buildings and employees, sitting on top of hundreds of years of history, and somehow trying to keep the whole thing afloat. The people who hold real power in the church are often (though not always) the most institutionalised people of all. Thus, much of our discussion, planning and use of energy becomes committed to maintaining the fabric and constitution of the church, rather than having a radical mission effect on the world around us. Possibly the two biggest issues in the life of the church over the last few years have been the ecumenical movement and the ordination of women. These are both essentially inward-looking institutional issues and secondary to the main theological direction of Christianity. The eventual outcome (if there ever is one) will have limited impact on the world, certainly on the world of the poor and needy.

The *Church Times*, which is meant to be a church newspaper, but is in fact a major part of and supporter of the institutional side of the church, recently carried a story entitled 'Significant Drop in Church of England Membership'. This was the most important story in the entire paper, yet it was tucked away on page eighteen. The front page was dominated by the really crucial church issues such as Hereford Cathedral selling off its treasures, and predictions about the make-up of the Lambeth Conference in 1998. This one little picture is a key to the broader picture of how the church as an institution sorts out its agenda. At national, diocesan, and local parish level the church devotes the bulk of its time and energy to internal institutional issues. In such an atmosphere, discussions, reports, committees, appointments, etc become endless, consuming huge mission resources. This atmosphere was captured beautifully by *The Independent* of November 11th, 1988. 'The general rule when trying to guess how the Synod will vote, is to work out which option entails putting off any decision for longest. That is the one that the Synod will choose.'

The Church of England, however, does not have a monopoly on institutionalism. The pattern of history is a repetition of religious revivals and powerful spiritual movements gradually being institutionalised: of energy being taken away from mission and committed to buildings and rituals; of large-scale bureaucracies replacing local leadership; and of inspired, often working-class, preachers and evangelists being gradually processed by middle-class academic training procedures. Thus the fire of the Wesleyans was turned to stone within a few generations. The Ranters, a new generation of fiery missioners, were formed out of Methodism, but gradually they also became fossilised. The same process has smitten the life of numerous movements over the years and is still happening today.

The church as a movement

The 'movement' side of the church is more concerned with what is happening out in the world than what is happening inside the church. It consists of everyone from Archbishops down to choirboys who look first to the world, to its need of Jesus, to its spiritual and material poverty, and then see themselves as part of the answer. Such people are a direct continuation of the coming of Jesus: they move out, just as he moved out, they encapsulate his message, his love and his power.

To expect the institutional side of the church to become an Apostolic Gospel, a bringer of life to the poor, is to invite continuous frustration and disillusionment. What can be done, however, and what will bear real fruit, is for Christians of goodwill to align themselves with the movement side of the church, to allow themselves to be guided, educated and inspired to 'move out', with others, into the spiritual wasteland.

The institutional side of the church is not just inhabited by dusty old traditionalists; there are actually lots of supposedly bouncy, dynamic radicals, charismatics and evangelicals within Anglicanism, Roman Catholicism, the Nonconformists and the modern House Movement, who are pure institutionalists. Conversely, there are thousands of Christians who at first glance appear to be classic traditionalists, but who in reality are blazingly alive church movement people.

The church becomes a movement when it moves. The church becomes the moving Jesus whenever someone steps outside the front door, walks across a piece of derelict wasteland, or a glass-showered children's playground and actually 'lives out' God to an inhabitant, not of the Holy City, but of the secular city.

The movement side of the church can be the means of renewal, revival and restoration of the whole church. Renewal people need to be willing to put their hands on the steering wheels (even when this means joining committees), in all corners of the church. Voices need to be raised, articles need to be written, votes need to be passed at every level. However, speaking as a committed, though at times impatient and unloving charismatic movement person, there are three things that I and others like me need to take to heart.

1. There are lots of institutional people who are genuinely thirsting for renewal. They must not be steam-rollered; they are individuals with something to receive and much to give.

2. The great sin of most movement people is that of a judgmental attitude. The evangelical charismatic movement is not identical to the full movement of God, it is a part of it. I have to avoid the tendency to pass quick judgements on everyone who does not think and act like me.

3. We must not throw the baby out with the bathwater. In this case

the baby is not nearly as big and healthy as it is supposed to be; nevertheless there are vital parts and aspects of the institution that need to be retained and revalued.

Institutional/movement tension

Jesus's parable of the tenants (Lk 20:9–19) established the insight that the old prophets had in fact been movement people who had proved too much for the institutional side of God's people to handle, and so they had been killed. Furthermore it was a prophecy that the same process would be responsible for his own death. This constant tension has led to many such suffocations throughout church history. However, the long-term decline of the church in this country means that in the late twentieth century the institution is in a new historical climate.

As the institutional side of the church continues to be worn down, through failure and apathy, so the growing, moving church will go on being an increasingly effective presence within it; funding it, staffing it and leading it.

The church at national, denominational and local level needs to be aware of the institutional/movement tension and to try and get the balance right. Too much institution and we turn into a museum, too much movement without an organisation and discipline and we become a wild forest fire.

A two-handed mission to the poor

When the movement side of the church moves into what man has made to be the second-class carriages of Bradford and the nation generally, it has to go in with a two-handed mission strategy. Such a strategy brings together what have often been called the 'social' and 'spiritual' gospels.

The social gospel attitude sees with a very clear eye that people are living in terrible housing conditions; that their children have little or no educational future; that the aged and disabled are brushed aside by the enterprise culture. It relates all these and similar issues to God's loving concern for every part of our lives, and then bases a mission strategy on the need for the church to reach out and do something practical and positive about such social evils.

Social gospel people tend to be very involved with community and maybe political compaigns, and usually come from a liberal or middle-of-the-road theological background.

The spiritual gospel attitude sees with an equally clear eye that people are living without Christ; that they have little or no experience of the joy of knowing God in this life, and nothing to look forward to in the future. It relates this to the love of God and the saving death of Christ, and then bases a mission strategy on the need for the church to reach out and tell people of Jesus and his gift of eternal life.

Spiritual gospel people tend to be very involved with congregational and maybe evangelistic campaigns, and usually come from an Evangelical or Anglo-Catholic theological background.

As soon as one sees the two attitudes side by side, one realises that it cannot be a question of 'either, or' but must be one of 'both, and'. Today a minority of Evangelicals are widening their outlook to take in issues of poverty, etc; in effect they are turning back to their true roots of the last century, when Evangelicals were very involved in the struggles for better housing, education, working conditions, etc. The majority, however, still retain a very narrow outlook and continue to be fully caught up in their own internal parochial affairs. Meanwhile the social gospel grouping in the churches often persists in condemning all others as not really caring. In the Church of England at national or diocesan levels, social gospel thinking is usually very strong and controls much of the planning and allocation of resources.

The Jesus gospel

The Jesus gospel holds together and actually puts into practice the social and the spiritual gospel. It represents the full depth and breadth of God's love, without missing anything out. It confronts sin and offers salvation in two overlapping zones, the corporate zone and the individual zone.

CORPORATE ZONE   INDIVIDUAL ZONE

Sin is rampant in our society, in the corporate zone: greed for money and power; political indifference; moral laxity; hardness of heart towards the vulnerable; racial, sexual and class prejudice all bring bitter consequences, especially for the poor, the handicapped, the aged, etc. Jesus hates this corporate sin and the pain it brings. The Jesus gospel brings judgement for the victimisers and compassion and healing for the victims, into this corporate zone.

Sin is not just prevalent in the corporate zone, it is also to be found in people's individual lives. The poor can be cruel, immoral and godless too, and being poor does not mean that God turns a blind eye. The Jesus gospel brings judgement against all evil, but it also offers forgiveness and salvation to all evil-doers who are prepared to change their ways and believe.

In the corporate zone the gospel represents a prophetic challenge to the structures and values of our society. It calls upon the rich and powerful to change or else. 'He has brought down rulers from their thrones but has lifted up the humble' (Lk 1:52).

In the individual zone it leads people into an experience of forgiveness, rebirth and eternal life. It binds up the broken and feeds the hungry. 'Come to me, all you who are weary and burdened, and I will give you rest' (Mt 11:28).

Jesus's ministry and life took him into both the corporate and the individual zones of humanity's plight. Where he leads the church should follow. The church nationally and denominationally must follow Jesus into the area of corporate sin with a clear and powerful prophetic gospel, which will challenge the victimisers and show love towards the victims. Parallel to this there has to be a major move towards the growth of local churches especially in the inner-city, and outer-city council estate areas. Healthy and loving churches here will bring the gospel into the individual zone of people's own sin and suffering. It will give the poor the opportunity at long last to discover the good news and the good caring love of their good God.

Homelessness is a good example of how the church can operate locally/individually and nationally/corporately. As a local church in an inner-city area we are increasingly involved in cases of homelessness. Sometimes we are able to find decent accommodation for people, at other times we have been able to take families away on short breaks, out of depressing conditions. Often we can do nothing about their housing or lack of it, but we can give food, clothing and day shelter. As well as this, however, we also try to tell folk about how our own sin estranges us from God, and how Jesus is able to forgive us and welcome us into an eternal and secure home. This sort of individual ministry can only happen when there is a healthy and growing local church.

This type of mission by itself, however, is not enough. It needs to be matched by the work of a national prophetic church. In an affluent society like ours, the existence of so many homeless is a corporate and national disgrace. The fact that there are now hundreds of thousands of people owning second houses and that local authorities hold millions of pounds from the sale of council houses which they are not allowed to use to build new ones turns the disgrace into a scandal. Furthermore, the housing shortage is made worse by the spreading decline of family life, as more families break into pieces, each of which need a house. The church needs to campaign with passion and unrelenting power, condemning those responsible for this area of corporate sin and siding with those suffering its consequences.

We can now examine in more detail the tasks of being a prophetic church, and a growing church.

Notes

1. John Atherton, *Faith in the Nation* (SPCK: London, 1988).
2. *The Legacy: The Challenge* (City of Bradford Metropolitan Council: 1986).

CHAPTER SEVEN

THE PROPHETIC CHURCH

The church throughout Britain, in rich, poor and in-between areas, desperately needs to be a church of prophecy: a church which speaks and acts prophetically to the world and also a church which itself hears and responds to the prophetic voice.

The role of the prophet is to be God's clear, loud and distinct mouthpiece, God's PA system breaking through the great clamouring babble of human thinking and discussion to reveal God's ideas, his wisdom and his judgements. Today the rich-poor divide in society, the decaying middle-class nature of the church, and the church's failure to be a church of the working classes, all call for a particularly powerful prophetic ministry.

The historical tradition of prophecy

Throughout the history of God's people, there has always been the need for men and women who were 'called', able and willing to take on the prophetic role.

Moses

Moses was the prototype of the great prophet/statesman/leader. He gave the Israelites directions in their wilderness wanderings; he gave great law codes to the emerging nation; he established a principle of being 'God's people'; fundamentally he kept the people in touch with God.

Samuel

In the early stages of Israel's history, Samuel took on the mantle and became their prophet/judge/priest. When the nation's actual existence was threatened by the Philistines he kept the flame of faith flickering; he helped the people resolve difficult dilemmas and spoke out God's will on the most momentous political and religious issue of his day, ie the setting up of the monarchy.

Nathan and Elijah

As the monarchy became ever more powerful, the role of the prophet became that of representing God at the king's court, of reminding him who the true king of Israel was, and of speaking up for the little man. Thus Nathan spoke out against David's taking of Bathsheba, and publicly rebuked the king. Later on God spoke and acted through the prophetic ministry of Elijah to challenge the entire political leadership of King Ahab.

The Canonical prophets

Economic progress for Israel and Judah brought prosperity for those at the top of the pile, but poverty, injustice and exploitation for those at the bottom. In this prevailing climate of the period from the eighth to the sixth centuries BC the job of the prophets Amos, Micah, Isaiah and Jeremiah, etc was to give voice to God's anger at the nation's social and economic evils, its religious hypocrisy and its crushing of the poor, and to warn of the coming judgement.

Jesus

The prophetic ministry of Jesus brought the words of God more clearly and more powerfully than ever before into the lives of God's people. His teachings were based on the laws of Moses and the prophetic tradition. His life, acts, healings and presence were a living challenge to those among whom he lived. As with most prophets he had to be silenced, rather than obeyed.

The New Testament

The New Testament situation was different from any which had gone before. God's people no longer constituted a nation with their own political leadership. Instead, they were a relatively small but growing community with a mission towards the nations. With the pouring out of the Spirit on all God's people at Pentecost, the gift of prophecy became more widespread. It is likely that there were people in most congregations with the 'calling' and the ability to deliver divine insight, guidance, correction and insight to God's people. Thus the intervention of the prophet Agabus in Acts 21 is accepted without question. Paul's listing of the 'word' ministries as the leading ministries in the church's life, groups prophecy alongside apostleship and teaching in 1 Corinthians 12. He encourages Christians to desire all spiritual gifts, but especially that of prophecy (1 Cor 14:1). The New Testament, and the Bible as a whole, is brought to an end with the climactic and prophetic book of Revelation.

Church history

Since the ending of the New Testament era the ministry of prophecy has often been allowed to lapse by the church, and there have been long periods of relative inactivity. Prophecy, however, never totally disappeared, as God continued to raise up men and women to speak out his words and thoughts. Sometimes this happened on a large international stage, eg Martin Luther, speaking out to restore biblical purity, enthusiasm and discipline in the church. Often prophecy continued in a much smaller and more limited context, eg Richard Oastler compaigning in West Yorkshire against the evils of child labour.

Prophetic pains

Despite the high profile given to prophecy in the Bible, prophets are often the most ignored, derided and openly abused people in the church. Jeremiah is perhaps the ultimate example of a sensitive man who found the prophetic ministry to be a source of great pain. He was horrified by his fellow prophets giving 'easy' messages of false comfort. He was pained by the lies and corruption of the priests. The vision of judgement and destruction in his mind caused him to experience the mourning of bereavement. He was hunted, imprisoned, almost murdered by his fellow Jews, and finally dragged off to Egypt, to die in a foreign land. No wonder he cried out to God with such anguish.

> Alas, my mother, that you gave me birth, a man with whom the whole land strives and contends! I have neither lent nor borrowed, yet everyone curses me (Jer 15:10).

> Whenever I speak, I cry out proclaiming violence and destruction. So the word of the Lord has brought me insult and reproach all day long. But if I say, 'I will not mention him or speak any more in his name,' his word is in my heart like a fire, a fire shut up in my bones. I am weary of holding it in; indeed, I cannot (Jer 20:8–9).

Jesus' parable of the tenants (Lk 20:9–17) dwells on the example of Jeremiah and the early prophets and concludes that rejection and death is the prophetic fate.

So the lone prophet, or the prophetic church which steps out looking for a fair hearing, a reasoned response or a mass positive repentance, is probably in for a rude awakening. It didn't happen then, and it will not happen now. Even within the church itself, most people from the highest down to the lowest like to hear nice comforting words, and tend to reject those that are too near the bone. For all of us the truth is often painful, but God's prophetic truth is creative of ultimate life and joy—'You will know the truth, and the truth will set you free.'

Prophecy today

In today's church prophecy is fashionable: virtually every Christian paperback that is published, and every well-known speaker who gets up to speak, is described as 'prophetic'. Rather than being the solitary lone voice of a few, the prophetic message today is chorused by multitudes. Today's prophet is a celebrity, a star performer in the church's line-up. In fact, as often happens, when a word is over-used it is over-abused. Much of today's talk of prophecy falls into one of two areas of distortion.

On the one hand, the liberal, social-gospel lobby in the church seems to applaud as prophetic anyone who strings together enough political cliches. The God who is supposed to be speaking through all of this, seems to have forgotten all about repentance leading to conversion and new life.

On the other hand, the charismatic lobby are in danger of trivialising prophecy, making it simply a string of pictures, feelings and words which supposedly always come from God. The God who is supposed to speak through all of this seems to have forgotten the biblical campaigns against social injustice.

Of course both positions contain some real prophetic insight, but they equally represent human distortion and manipulation of what belongs to God. True prophecy holds together essential religious truths and convictions with their social, economic and political implications. True prophecy has both a large-scale application to nations, cities and churches, and also a limited and personal application to individuals and small groups.

Much of today's prophecy is concerned with 'them over there'; thus prophecy coming from a left-wing political group will be aimed at telling 'them over there' in a right-wing group how terrible they are. Similarly there is a rising chorus of prophetic statements coming out of the house church and the Restoration movement telling 'them over there' in the other denominations how spiritually dead they are.

Biblical prophecy does have a word for 'them over there'. Amos's book of prophecy begins by speaking out against Israel's foreign neighbouring countries; the prophet Jonah was sent to the Assyrian capital of Nineveh; and Jeremiah had much to say against the nation of Babylon. However, this speaking out against someone else is relatively limited when compared with the prophetic utterances against 'us over here'. The vast bulk of biblical prophecy was intended for internal consumption: God using a human mouthpiece to speak first and foremost to his own people, nation, church, that they might put their own life in order before speaking out to others. In other words, a prophet does not throw stones at other people's greenhouses. The best prophets are usually committed 'insiders', caring passionately about the church, city or country to which they have been called by God to speak prophetically.

The prophetic task

Amos, himself a prophet, gives a very useful description of the prophetic task, as someone who is called and charismatically equipped to receive and then transmit God's plans (Amos 3:7–8). To this we can add Oscar Cullman's very helpful definition of the job of the prophet:

'He explains to the people the true meaning of all events; he informs them of the plan and will of God at the particular moment.' If this task is to be carried out properly then there has to be a two-part prophetic process. Using the metaphor of J. V. Taylor in *The Go-Between God* the prophet is not only a radio transmitter, he is also a radio receiver.[1] He has to take in, and understand before he can explain and give out.

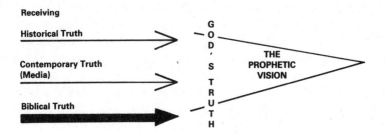

Historical truth

A prophet needs to have a nose for history. We cannot understand the present without understanding the past. History helps
us to understand why people act and believe as they do, why
society is the shape it is, and what part the church has played in all
of this. If certain ideas are being tried or put into operation today,
eg the government's *laissez-faire* free-market economy, history
can show us where similar ideas were tried in the past.

A rather cynical interpretation of history is 'the only thing we
learn from the past is that we learn nothing from the past.' The
great prophets of Israel, including Jesus, were all students of
history; they were continually referring people back in order to
understand where things were going to in the future.

Contemporary truth

Our main source of information for what is actually going on
today is the media. The media, by and large, are owned and
controlled by a small group of people who have their own
philosophy and values. The newspapers and TV channels which
they own tend to reflect their views. In effect, their prejudice has
become a very powerful opinion-former in the minds of millions.

In exactly the same way most of our newspapers are very supportive of Conservative politics, and of the style of leadership which was for so long associated with Margaret Thatcher. This is not surprising, for the people who own and run these papers are generally very affluent and have most to gain from such politics. These same papers are usually insulting or at best patronising to the poor; often sexist and regularly racist, they hate the church when it is doing its job and love it when it is being a safe traditional institution. This media machine fills the minds of millions, including many Christians and Christian leaders, with its godless propaganda and misinformation.

The prophetic seeker-after-truth needs to close his mind to much of this outpouring, but he does need to be well informed. There is a strand of the media which is still struggling to pass on truthful information, expose cover-ups, point the finger at hypocrisy and ask the awkward questions. This strand of contemporary reporting, art, and social science is a friend and vital ingredient of the prophetic vision. However, this 'truth strand' is itself under pressure; for example, the BBC, a world-acclaimed news service offering accurate and generally neutral information, is coming under mounting attacks from powerful politicians.

The person or church who wants fully to understand the day's events will feed on good newspapers, TV documentaries, investigative radio programmes, modern dramas, poetry and literature, and the fruit of much careful sociological and psychological research. That is not to say they will simply swallow everything; they will not be naive or undiscerning in their reading and ultimately they will want to measure everything by the yardstick of the Bible.

Biblical truth

The third major input to the prophetic reception and understanding process is the Bible itself. If the prophet's task is to deliver the particular and contemporary word of God, then that word should spring from, and be guided by, the revealed word of God.

For many Christians involved in the political world, the strongest influence on their minds is their respective political ideology; they are Socialist, Liberal or Conservative first, and Christian second. Yet for the true Christian the Bible should be the first influence on every part of our thinking, be it political, social, personal, spiritual, philosophical or moral. For the Christian, the Bible is a life manifesto.

Prophecy is about clear understanding. Biblical light clears away the confused ideas of our own political ideology; it clears away mass-media propaganda; it clears away left-wing intellectual propaganda; it clears away the prejudices we have picked up on our path through life from parents, teachers, friends, etc. It presents a clear vision of people living together in community, learning to depend on each other, living with God at the heart of their society, living along the lines of justice, compassion and equality.

Many Christians read the parts of the Bible they agree with. They distort the Bible to make it fit with their mind, rather than changing their mind to make it fit in with the Bible. Thus left-wingers pick out the red bits, social-gospel people pick out the social bits, evangelicals pick out the evangelistic bits, charismatics pick out the Holy-Spirit bits and Conservatives pick out what they think are the blue bits. But the Bible is not a box of 'all-sorts', with everybody's favourite bits: all of us need to read and obey all of the Bible.

Prophetic insight is not born out of a mystical trance-like experience of the supernatural, although it should involve an aspect of this. Essentially it is the fruit of a disciplined, broad-fronted receptiveness and study. Through the disciplines of history, contemporary studies and biblical analysis the prophetic mind becomes engaged with God's living truth.

Transmitting

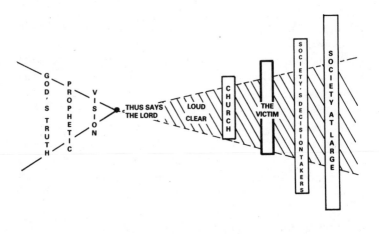

Powerful transmission

God's word is a word that goes out to touch human life. The prophetic church becomes part of this process when it proclaims its prophetic vision with loudness and clarity. The prophetic word needs to speak to the perpetrators of injustice, and to the victims of injustice.

The perpetrators of injustice, be they religious leaders, politicians, powerful figures in the worlds of commerce or business, or decision-makers in the media, education or the arts, etc, all need to know that the church is not on their side, that what they are doing is wrong in the eyes of a loving God of justice, and that their activities will eventually lead to judgement. Not only have many of these people never felt the church's attack in the past— many of them, or their equivalents, have actually enjoyed our active support: eg many of the industrialists and politicians who were committed to *laissez-faire* economies and the evils it led to in the last century were supported by Anglicanism.

Not all of society's leaders and decision makers are 'the enemy' however (although simply belonging to a church does not make someone an ally and part of the true prophetic vision; there are many politicians today producing plenty of Christian words but few Christian works). There are people in influential positions in every walk of life who will welcome and respond positively to an intelligent prophetic voice. Furthermore, there are many in various situations who will be forced to respond, if the prophetic voice has the right effect on their electors and customers.

The victims of injustice are the powerless and the voiceless; they have no contacts, no money power, no influence, no united strong voice that anyone is going to listen to. They wonder if anyone really knows what it is like; if anyone cares; they wonder if God knows or cares.

A truly prophetic church, a church which really gets alongside people, which prefers incarnation to patronisation, will show the people that yes, we do care, and that no, God has not forgotten them. I was recently involved in a march by Christians, in protest against government attempts to introduce charges for eye and dental check-ups. Most people just couldn't understand why we were bothering about an everyday non-Christian issue. They were used to us campaigning to 'Keep Sunday Special' or to maintain religious education in schools; these were 'our sort' of issue in which we had a vested interest. Many were bemused by it all, but some were challenged by the sight of a prophetic church showing genuine concern. After the march I received various letters and phone calls from non-Christians and in one or two cases people had actually been brought closer to God by the event.

The voice needs to go out with power and clarity; it needs to be loud and clear. The church, especially the Church of England, is expert at producing 'good-taste' prophecy, and remaining 'cool under the collar'. We write letters to the quality press or our MPs, we have rational debates in our Diocesan Synods, and everything is done in the best of English using articulate and erudite arguments. Our attacks are cushioned with cautious qualifications, displomatic decency and an apologetic air.

The prophets of Israel were obedient to God, concerned for the exploited, and apologetic to no one. We can learn from their passion, from the rawness of their language, from their ability to communicate with telling images, such as Isaiah's 'heroes of the wine bottle' (Is 5:22) and Micah's 'wealthy stripping the flesh off the bones of the poor' (Mic 3:2–3), from their simple and emphatic phrases. One of the reasons for the subtle and sophisticated prophecy of today, relates to the middle-class make-up of Christian leadership. Many of the people leading the church today went to school with, are members of the same club as, and are fellow socialisers of the decision makers, the power-brokers of our cities and nation. Our leadership consists generally, though not entirely, of 'nice' people. I can think of many adjectives to describe Amos or John the Baptist, but I can't think of any less appropriate than the word 'nice'.

Amos was a lowly man from a working-class background, and raised up by God. His prophetic message was so loud and clear that the priest Amaziah had to work with the king to try to get rid of him. Today, there are increasing signs that key leaders of society are getting rattled and angry with the churches, especially with the Church of England. They are using their own people who are members of the church to infiltrate and divert us from our true calling; they are looking for opportunities to penetrate and speak at major church gatherings where they re-interpret Scripture to suit their own viewpoint, they use crude half-veiled threats such as loss of funding, etc. Thus in 1988 the then Prime Minister went along to the Church of Scotland to tell them what Christianity was really all about. Meanwhile, south of the border key cabinet ministers tried to do the same, while John Selwyn Gummer continued to occupy an interesting dual role as a government minister and an outspoken member of the General Synod. If Labour were in power there would be a need for a prophetic church to speak out against some of their actions too, and presumably they would engage in similar tactics to frighten, divert and silence such a church.

Prophecy to the church

Of course it is not just the secular principalities and powers that are disturbed by and disobedient to the prophetic word. There have been two major attempts in this century to shift the Church of England into an evangelistic 'growth mode'. The first was in 1917 when the Archbishop set up a special Committee of Enquiry, the second came in 1945 with the publication of *Towards the Conversion of England*. The institution however managed to resist both attacks.

As I write we are still in the early days of the 'Decade of Evangelism'. There are already clear signs of a 'prophetic power versus immovable object' struggle going on. The decade is of vital importance to the future of churches of all denominations, and through them, to the future of our whole society. Some of the lessons to be learnt from the history of the Church of England in the nineteenth century is that it is possible for a huge institution to take evangelism seriously and to go from a 'maintaining things as they are' frame of mind, to a 'we must reach out' frame of mind. The results then were amazing as membership increased fourfold over a sixty-year period. If it happened then it can happen now, and to all the churches. There is a battle to be fought, however: the cynics, the institutionalisers and the theologically misguided must not be allowed to triumph as they often have in the past.

The report *Faith in the City*, published in 1985, is perhaps the ultimate modern example of organised Christians attempting to carry out a prophetic enquiry and proclamation. It looked at the life and the likely future of the church, and of society generally. In particular it looked at poverty, unemployment, housing, health, social care, education and law and order. It combined good historical analysis with much contemporary information and incorporated penetrating biblical social principles.

Its discussion of the problems facing the church contained some careful and probing analysis, although as is often the case, its thoughts on evangelism and church growth were minimal. In fact, of thirty-eight recommendations to the church, not one mentions this area of mission at all. Its work on social and economic issues, however, was its strong point, and was highly acclaimed by people working in the respective areas who were not themselves members of the church.

Thus the process of receiving, of gathering information and trying to understand it was very well done. When it came to transmission, however, the exercise failed miserably, despite the modern myth of *Faith in the City*. The myth is that the church is supposed to have published a report amid a burst of publicity, which had government ministers quaking in their boots, and which has since gone on to massive and profound effects on the life of the Church of England. In fact it was members of the government who first leaked it to the press: the first many people heard of it was the voice of Norman Tebbit on Radio Four quoting it as another example of Socialist/Marxist infiltration of the Church of England. Church dignitaries, by comparison, appeared to be almost embarrassed by the whole episode. The publicity battle was lost before it was begun, and there were soon signs of smiling compromises between church and government ministers.

Today we have a Church Urban Fund—admittedly dwarfed by the amount the church spends on its twenty-eight cathedrals, but still it is there, and it is better than nothing. Of the other thirty-eight recommendations to the church and twenty-three recommendations to the nation, little is now heard.

Thank God that there are today a growing number of major Christian prophets around: John Wimber, with a message of spiritual renewal to the churches; Jim Wallis, whose words bring the real pain of compassion to all who hear and read them; Desmond Tutu, the ultimate genuinely caring critic of his political overlords; Trevor Huddleston, David Sheppard, David Jenkins and the recently retired Archbishop of Canterbury.

So the church is becoming a prophetic church, but there is much still to be done; much apathy, cynicism, naivety and one-sidedness to be swept away. As this happens the world will see, feel and hear the prophet Jesus from Nazareth.

Note

1. John Taylor, *The Go-Between God* (SCM: London, 1972).

CHAPTER EIGHT

THE GROWING CHURCH

Ultimately 'the church' means the local church congregation, the group of people drawn out of a community and meeting to worship God, and to channel his love and message out into the world. The greatest single need in the church's mission to the poor today is for a large number of small, struggling and slowly dying churches to be re-ignited into qualitive and quantitive growth. The poor need to have the opportunity to find Jesus and enter into his salvation for themselves. Realistically this is only going to happen when the local church in the inner-city and in the outer-city council estates is alive with God and in touch with people.

Eight years ago I was invited to become vicar of St Augustine's, Otley Road, Bradford. At the time it was the last place on earth I wanted to go to; however, I had a very sure sense that it was where God wanted me to be. I arrived with a heavy heart, not really knowing where to start. In my weakness all I could do was cast myself onto God and trust in his guidance and strength.

At the time St Augustine's was on the point of closure. It was a huge Victorian barn built to seat 1100 people, with a small but very committed congregation. Everything that could go wrong with a building had gone wrong with St Augustine's: dry rot, wet rot, freezing temperatures and a leaking roof which meant that on rainy days there were more buckets than people in church. The parish consisted mainly of 'Coronation Street' terraces and sixties and seventies council developments, with a large Asian community.

Today I look back and see just how much growth God has produced in the church. Our adult membership has risen to about 250 and is still growing; our life of worship, fellowship, evangelism and social concern is joyful, positive and wonderfully united. We have replaced our old church with a new multi-purpose building open seven days a week. This houses a local library, a Christian café and various community activities meeting the needs of local people. We have opened a community centre in the most deprived part of the parish and we are just in the process of starting up a second morning service designed specifically to touch local non-churchgoing working-class people. There are still large disappointments: we have been unable to make much headway into the local Asian population, and we are struggling with our children's and youth evangelism.

There are of course lots of more exciting church growth projects than St Augustine's, and we are certainly not fully content and satisfied with what has been achieved so far. Nevertheless there is much in our story to show that God is desiring and able to lead small churches in the most depressing situations into times of growth.

The gospel is a productive seed: if it is planted in the right way, in the right conditions and nurtured by the right sort of fingers then it will grow. Many of our churches however are overgrown with weeds, equipped with rusty and ill-used implements, while many of the gardeners are pessimistic and don't really expect much to grow. Many don't even bother to plant the seed, but leave it in the sack to gather dust. If the seed is to grow the ground needs to be cleared of much ecclesiastical rubbish and cultural weeds; it needs to be planted afresh with skill and conviction in the lives first of all of the churchgoers themselves. Once planted it needs to be fed, watered and nurtured with deep prayer and good practices. Most important of all, the gardeners need to have a renewed optimism and positive belief in the purpose and outcome of their planting.

It is essential that this new beginning be based on evangelistic effectiveness, for two reasons. Firstly, the poor have been denied Jesus for too long. To give someone Jesus is to give them the best and most valuable part of creation's life. Put crudely, the working classes have never had their fair share of God. They need and deserve people telling them how and why they can begin a new and eternal life. There are people in our church suffering long-term from all sorts of social deprivation issues which we have not been able to resolve. However, in introducing them to Jesus we have opened up their lives to a whole new and joyful future, and we have drawn them into a loving and caring community called the church of Jesus Christ.

Secondly, the church nationally is haemorrhaging. We are losing members at an alarming rate. This applies particularly but not exclusively to working-class areas. We are reaching the point where we just do not have the members to carry out any sort of effective mission, be it social or spiritual. Unless we rediscover the ability to produce new Christians in substantial numbers we will soon virtually disappear. This in no way discredits the importance of social-gospel work; it merely argues pragmatically that in the immediate future our main priority must be evangelistic growth.

When I first came to St Augustine's there were people who expected me to launch all sorts of programmes, but I had to push these expectations to one side and be single-minded. It was crucial that we set out to produce first and foremost about twenty adult converts. Once the church began to grow numerically the whole morale of the congregation increased. We became stronger qualitatively and quantitively and then, and only then, could we begin to diversify and slowly develop other programmes. (Sadly it has to be said that some churches never move outside this single goal of seeking individual converts, and forget all about people's wider social needs.) John Wimber gives a very good piece of advice to all small churches that want to grow. He tells them to just do one or two new things, but to do them very well.

Numerical church growth comes from four areas:

Biological growth — church families having babies.

Transfer growth — people joining from other churches, for all manner of reasons, some good, some bad.

Restoration growth — members who have fallen away being reclaimed.

Conversion growth — non-Christians being converted and discipled.

All these areas are important, but if we are to reach the 'unchurched' masses then restoration and conversion growth are particularly important.

A strategy for the growth of small churches

We will soon reach a point (if we have not already reached it) where the majority of churches of all denominations will be small churches, ie a listed membership of less than fifty. The very expression 'small church' is to many a painful one, carrying connotations of failure, decline and poor standards. However, if we throw away such connotations and forget our bloated memories of a 'golden past', and if we ignore the noises of success coming from other bigger churches (which are often more of a discouragement than an encouragement), we can approach the equation in a more positive light. Thus thirty or forty people meeting regularly with a capable and trained leader can suddenly be seen as a very powerful launch pad from which to project church growth. Such a church can be an excellent and growing fellowship full of joy and power.

Roy Pointer lists three particular advantages of a small church.[1]

> It can concentrate in an especially rich way on the basics of word and sacrament.
>
> It can have a very real sense of unity and fellowship, into which new people find access much easier than in a large church.
>
> The scale of commitment and ministry of the laity is likely to be much higher than in a bigger church where 'someone else will always do it'.

At St Augustine's today, some of the earliest converts from eight years ago actually look back to when we were a very small church in an old building. They see that past time as a very special period in our church's history, when there was a struggling but very warm atmosphere.

There is today a small but growing number of such churches scattered across the country. They are often situated in the most inhospitable settings, but are experiencing real growth, both qualitative and quantitative. It is possible to extrapolate from their success a 'small church growth strategy'. This strategy is based on five steps or stages:

1. The adoption of positive, faith-based attitudes.
2. The making of radical changes in the lifestyle, routine and general outlook of the local church, changing from being the 'local parish church or chapel', to becoming a 'local mission church or chapel'.
3. The creation of an alive and attractive Sunday worship event.
4. The establishing of a church family life based on the sharing of prayer, Bible study and the fullness of life.
5. The receiving of the right sort of outside support.

Leadership

At each of these stages the leader or minister plays a key part; in fact, after the Holy Spirit, the quality of the church's leadership is the most important single ingredient in producing church growth.

One of the key factors leading to church growth in the nineteenth century was good leadership. In the Primitive Methodist and Salvation Army tradition, the leaders were working class, enthusiastic and with high levels of expectant faith. In the Church of England, many of the clergy experienced deep spiritual renewal producing a strong sense of vocation, prayer and service. The priests of the Roman Catholics were drawn from the same Irish rural background as their congregations, and they had the feel of the people. If these strains could be brought together in the churches in working-class areas today, we would have a spiritually powerful, visionary and gifted leadership, able to understand and communicate with the local culture.

Ten years ago the Partners in Mission Consultation took a long, hard look at the Church of England. Their excellent report, *To a Rebellious House*, produced some painful but necessary observations. This is what they said then about the clergy.

> In order to prepare clergy for the Church you must have a clear vision of what it means to be a believer in 1981, of the role of the Church community and of the function of the clergy within it. The quality of the Church depends upon the quality of its responsible pastors. In the Church of England such a clear vision seems to be absent: the laity, from whom the clergy are drawn, are confused when confronted with conflicting and contrasting lifestyles in neighbouring parishes and dioceses, and later also in contrasting (and perhaps conflicting) theological colleges. Post-ordination training, apparently without continuity, continues the absence of a clear vision of the role of the clergy within the Church.[2]

These words apply equally to clergy of all denominations, and they are more urgent now than they were in 1981.

My own personal reflections on some success and lots of mistakes provoke three main comments. Firstly, leaders need a vision from God, a goal, a new land, towards which they will journey, for without a vision the people perish (Prov 29:18). This has to be a realistic vision, one which is attainable but not easy.

Secondly, leaders must lead and not stand still. Leadership involves stepping out in faith, often at the front, and this is painful, frightening and can be lonely at times. The alternative is to stand still, to reflect the status quo, to pander to the desires of the non-moving elements in our congregation.

Thirdly, as leaders we must be constantly trying to improve our own gifts and abilities. Of course we can't get better at everything all the time. In recent years I have concentrated on three areas. I have worked at my ability to lead people individually to Christ. I have tried to sharpen up my preaching of sermons which call for a decision. Finally, I have attempted to widen my general awareness of community life and to become more informed about the dynamics, the needs and the various agencies all operating within it.

Spiritual leadership, however, should never become spiritual dictatorship. Leadership will always involve some separateness, but this need not be isolation. The Pauline picture of the church as the body of Christ, with the Holy Spirit distributing his gifts among the membership, opens the way for shared leadership. A leader of even the smallest and humblest fellowship will find maybe two or three people who can take tasks on board, with whom he can talk and gradually open their vision. Such leadership chrysalides will probably have to be helped if they are to form a praying, sharing leadership cell. One of my biggest failings over the years has been in this area of sharing leadership with lay leaders. I should have spent more time than I have in giving them thorough training, careful briefings and patient pastoring. At times I have resented having to share my power and influence with them. The high quality of lay leadership that has emerged says much more about them than it does about me. Shared leadership is not about shared privilege, or shared badge-wearing, but about shared responsibility and servanthood. Worldly leadership patterns establish the leader at the top of a pyramid. Christ's example of servanthood reverses the principle.

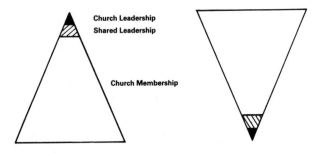

Thus the leader or leaders of a church are the feet washers. They cannot ask the church to enter into any experience, change or commitment until they have first entered into it themselves. Thus they lead the way into the five strategy steps; they lead the way into a deeper experience of the Holy Spirit; and they lead the way into sacrificial giving; they lead the way into shared open prayer.

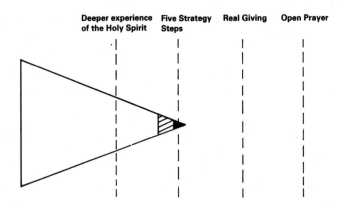

Strategy and the Spirit

Strategy, that is to say a good plan of action that is likely to lead to success, is not a substitute for the Spirit; it is rather a tool of the Spirit. Our plans, our leadership, our membership, traditions, buildings, liturgy and everything about us as the church is simply a huge pile of bones until the Spirit breathes life into and inhabits us. Until we are willing and desperate enough to open up to the Spirit, a good strategy will merely be an attempt to sew a new patch onto an old wine-skin.

Similarly the Spirit is not a substitute for strategy. It is not enough simply to be filled with the Spirit and then to turn up and smile at people. The picture of Jesus's ministry and of that of the apostolic church is that of sound strategies, careful thought and planning. Preparation and planning need not stifle spontaneity and freedom; they can actually be a springboard and safeguard. These five strategic steps are all based on biblical principles; furthermore they are principles which have been revealed afresh by the Spirit as he moves today in his church.

Positive attitudes

People who are confident, positive and optimistic have a much fuller experience of the whole of life. Their fullness of living rubs off on others; they tend to get things done. When this human optimism becomes grounded in living faith in the living God then the chemistry is even more explosive.

Too many churches and too many church leaders are pessimistic and negative with stunted little aspirations and hopes. Is it any wonder we achieve so little, when we believe in and expect so little? This first strategic step for church growth is to start to become faithful, positive people. Of course, straight away the chorus goes up 'but it's not that easy', 'people are what they are, and can't suddenly make themselves something else', 'not everyone can be an extrovert', etc. All of these and many others are valid comments, expressing genuine fears. The speed with which they sometimes spring forth indicates that there is often a deeply underlying negative, faults-finding attitude. I myself am, by nature, an extremely insecure, doubting and unsure person; for many years I have experienced great pain and disillusionment, in my personal life and in my ministry. Despite this, however, I have also experienced something totally alien to my nature. The inner healing of God, added to my own God-inspired determination, added again to my personal faith and commitment to optimism, have nurtured an increasingly positive attitude to life.

I have added this personal note as an encouragement. I know that if positive attitudes can grow in me, they can grow in anyone. Faith and positivism have affected not only my ministry, but my whole experience of life. These attitudes are not easy to nourish; there are numerous snakes to slide down as well as ladders to climb, but they are essential.

Today's clergy training, both at college and in service, places great emphasis on skills; but Jesus's training of his disciples was much more about faith and belief and positively going out for a goal. We seem simply to assume that everyone already has strong faith, and pass over it in our haste to hand on management skills, spirituality programmes, evangelistic techniques and theological awareness. Of course, all these are important, but the best gardening technique and toolbox is useless, unless the gardener has a powerful optimistic expectation of what he is doing. Most of us need careful and gentle outside help to acquire it.

The first strategic step towards growth is for the leader of the small church to adopt positive, faith-based attitudes. For most leaders this is a painful and soul-searching process. Many of us need a good outsider to teach, encourage, and even pump their positive belief into us. The leader can then begin, through preaching, pastoral visits, and group work, to lead his leaders and congregation, one by one, into a positive and faith-based outlook on life. Faith and positivism are essentially communal experiences which increase through giving to others and receiving back.

In our early days at St Augustine's I began to nurture my

relationship with a few of the key lay people and their partners (where this applied). I sensed their positive hopefulness beginning to feed off mine and to grow. As one or two good things began to happen in church (eg the worship and teaching improved), a few new faces appeared, and their positive hopefulness became much less dependent on me and much more dependent on God. Quite soon we were in a position where, when my positive attitudes collapsed occasionally, I was able to feed off them.

The adoption of positive attitudes, based not on ourselves or each other, but upon faith in God, is the beginning of growth.

Of course, sweeping out negativism does not mean sweeping out realism, and being a positive person does not mean being positive about everything. There are lots of areas of failure, bad practice, second-rate habits and untrue beliefs in all the churches. Then the prophetic outlook speaks strongly and critically against what is bad, and wants to get rid of it.

A local mission church

Commenting on the Church of England's attitude to evangelism the Partners in Mission report said:

> The Church suffers from the lack of a sense of urgency in evangelism. Its clergy are pastorally not evangelistically orientated, particularly due to their statutory roles as state baptisers, marriers and buriers. This leaves little time for the proclamation of the gospel or for their being enablers of the lay people in mission.[3]

Churches, and most church leaders, are habitually conservative, clinging to the past, and to that with which we feel secure and comfortable. Over the years a picture has developed of what the local church or chapel is all about; how its life should be ordered; its daily, weekly and yearly routine; the roles of its clergy and leading lay people, etc. The picture is in fact about what is the 'done thing'. Many are desperate to hang on to this picture; even many leaders, often in key strategic positions, are hugely over-cautious and tied to the past.

'Christian' England

The painful truth is that the traditional package is a failed package; it has been failing for over three hundred years. The Church of England has experienced only one significant growth period since the Reformation, and that was in the second half of the nineteenth century. There has been minor growth, eg some evangelical revival growth in the late eighteenth century, and some increase of attendance among middle-class churchgoers after the Second World War. In the main, then, we can say that the church is suffering from a 300-year-old terminal disease. If the traditional way of doing things, conducting services, training clergy, etc, was a good way, then we wouldn't be bleeding to death.

In trying to discover an accurate and up-to-date picture of national church trends, probably the best place to look is *'Christian' England*, the report by Peter Brierley of the 1989 English Church Census.[4] This book is crammed with helpful statistics, diagrams and suggestions, and among its many conclusions it reveals the following:

> Between 1975 and 1989 every single year 28,000 adults and 19,000 children in England stopped going to church.

> Between 1979 and 1989 adult membership of the English churches declined overall by 3%. This decline was particularly marked for the United Reformed Church (-18%), Roman Catholic (-14%), Methodist (-11%) and Anglican (-9%).

> Adult churchgoing is declining fastest in city centres and inner-city areas, and among Anglo-Catholic and 'Broad Church' attenders.

> Between 1979 and 1989 a local church closed down somewhere in England, every single week. However, there is still one church left to every 1,200 head of population, a very strong base from which to launch growth.

Over a third (34%) of all adult churchgoers in England live in the suburban/urban fringe. The inner cities and council estates combined can only account for 17%.

Between 1985 and 1989, 25% of all English churches grew. The highest proportion of these growing churches were Charismatic/Evangelical (41%).

These figures need not frighten us (especially if we are being positive), but they should stimulate, provoke and generally kick us up the trousers. The churches are like a well-known chain store with branches all over the country that is sliding towards bankruptcy; either we change or go bust. The church institutions are far too big and tortoise-like to make significant changes, but individual churches which are sliding towards bankruptcy need to be ruthlessly truthful with themselves, need to cut through all the sentiment of tradition, face up to the failure and make the right sort of changes, not in a rush but at good speed.

This 'truth interrogation' process needs to start with the leaders, who will need sensitive and trustworthy assistance to look at their own practices and their original training, but the system that trained them has been failing for a long time, especially in working-class areas.

The small struggling church which wants to go forward into growth needs to drop its attempt at being the parish church. To be the parish church needs lots of people, a good choir and plenty of males; even then it often doesn't work. This parish church personality needs to be replaced by a mission church one where freedom with discipline, spontaneity balanced by sound planning and flexibility within a good framework are the order of the day. The mission church needs to have the courage to try new things, and to go on trying even after flops and failures. It needs to stop ploughing energy into the traditional channels and divert it instead into mission. It means that the minister stops being the parish priest and in effect becomes the community missioner.

At St Augustine's this changeover from being a normal parish church to becoming a local mission church began in a moment of painful truthfulness. When there was talk of the church being closed down, suddenly all the illusions and the cobwebs were cut through in a flash. People realised that things had to change and became personally willing to allow change. The choice was between growth or death. If the church had died then it would have been one more working-class community losing one of its main links with God.

This process of facing up to the facts is an essential step for any church. It can begin by looking back over attendance figures, membership rolls, and rates of giving compared to inflation, etc. It can be useful to discover everybody's age and work out percentages. The results of all this digging can be collected, represented in a series of graphs and pie charts and used as a basis for future projections. The leader can work on this process with his key lay leaders, and they together can then present their findings first to the main church committee, secondly to the core membership and finally to the congregation. It's important that a true picture based on real facts is presented. The chances are that such a presentation will be painful in the short term, galvanising in the medium term and fruitful in the long term. Members will probably be frightened at first, but will then start to say 'Well, what can we do about it?', and will soon move on to say 'Well, let's get on and do it, then.'

The local mission church must move away from the institutional 'Maintaining things as good as we can, for as long as we can' mentality, to a 'Let's go out and take Jesus to the world' mentality. The new 'mission mentality' thus produced needs to be channelled by positive faith-based leadership into good mission practices. As a guide for those of us trying to formulate such good practices, church-growth thinkers have produced a very useful model based on the three 'P's.

Presence   — The church has to be where the people are, sharing
                their lives and establishing a presence which has

integrity and permanency. This presence establishes the platform for our proclamation.

Proclamation — Through its life, its events and its activity the church has got to proclaim, announce and somehow get across to local people the essential gospel message.

Persuasion — Having proclaimed the message, the church has got to engage people in a dialogue. By acts of love and practical concern, through friendship and through purposeful conversion we must try to persuade those whose interest has been aroused by our proclamation, that the message is true.

Initial phase

There are people close to every church, congregation and minister who are relatively open to the gospel, with whom good bridges have already been built. Before diverting energy to the long-term task of building bridges with those distant from the church, initial attention can be fruitfully directed to these close contacts, eg

- people who have recently left the church, perhaps during a previous incumbency;
- occasional attenders;
- strangers who simply 'turn up' for odd reasons or no reason;
- friends and family of those already committed;
- people who receive a church magazine or attend the annual Spring Fair or bazaar, etc;
- those who come to us for baptism, weddings, funerals;
- interested parents of Sunday school children, etc.

Even a small church will have a significant number of such 'fringe contacts'. The majority of these will never become Christians, but a goodly number will, if the good news is presented by a patient, caring and capable person. Such a person should not be a recruiting sergeant, or a spiritual head-hunter, but a giver-away of eternal life.

In the initial phase of work at St Augustine's I viewed myself as an urban missionary, and I made a beeline for all these fringe people. I chatted to them, visited them and asked questions to discover where they were at spiritually. When it became clear that they were not interested in going any deeper into God I graciously moved on, while remaining on good terms. On the other hand when I discovered that one of them was responding positively I spent time working with them to encourage them to faith. Slowly they came in one by one. After a time it was possible to train and use lay people in this careful one-to-one evangelism of warm contacts.

Follow-on phase

As this first stage mission strategy begins to bear fruit, the range of the 'going out movement' can be broadened and deepened.

It may be right to identify one or two local community needs and to set up a practical programme to do something about them. At St Augustine's my wife got a few church women together with one or two of their friends and set up a 'Parent and Toddler' group. I and two members of the church got very involved in the work of our local school.

A few months into our evangelism programme we started organising one or two large-scale social events. These gave our growing, confident congregation and our few new converts the chance to invite people to something that was good and enjoyable.

There is a need to develop a two-pronged approach to evangelism. One is spontaneous evangelism, the everyday sharing and witnessing by all Christians. We continually prod and encourage each other to be daily witnesses; we preach about it, pray about it, ask people to make short lists of their positive contacts, etc. The second prong is programmed evangelism, ie a well-planned series of occasional evangelistic events. Guest services, men's pub evenings, mini-missions, leafleting campaigns and outdoor services are just a few of the many ways of making our presence felt and sounding our proclamation throughout an area.

These sorts of programmed evangelistic activities are not just for urban and suburban churches. In his book *Strategies for Rural Evangelism* Chris Edmondson gives some practical suggestions, designed specifically for churches in the country and rural churches.[5] These include 'Songs of Praise'; using church buildings that are attractive and open all day; festivals and special occasions; small home groups; going into village pubs. He also discusses children's work, evangelism training and missions, all in a rural context.

Thus the initial work slowly develops as gradually more people are involved. In this way the presence is established, the proclamation is heard and the work of persuasion is patiently entered into.

When the non-Christians' interest has been aroused by the presence of Christians, and they have experienced an initial proclamation of the message, the work of persuasion begins. This process can take different forms. Some people are actually persuaded by the earliest proclamation and make a profession of faith after a first conversation or at an evangelistic event. Most, however, will need further discussions with the Christian friend who originally brought them along, or with a counsellor or minister. There are various strategies and training programmes to enable churches to improve their persuasion skills. Evangelism Explosion and 'The Gospel Down Your Street', as pioneered by Michael Wooderson, are two such.[6] We have three main systems for helping interested or searching people to find faith. Some are looked after by the clergy or a capable lay person. Others are invited to have a series of home studies with a team of two or three lay people leading basic Christianity sessions in the person's own home. Thirdly, we run short introductory group studies, which we usually call 'foundations' or 'basics', into which we gather about six people.

In the initial stages the minister may have to be a one-person mission unit; he or she may need training, encouragement and fellowship with other one-person mission units. Taking the vital decision to stop being the parish priest and to start being the local missioner calls for courage and help, but it is the step that needs to be taken by lots of church leaders in the near future. Those that don't take this sort of step, who feel threatened or perhaps angered by such ideas and who prefer the traditional model, will have to have very good reasons for believing that a system that has failed everywhere (especially in working-class areas) will work well in theirs.

Sunday worship

The most crucial and vital thing that happens in the life of any church is its average, bread and butter, Sunday worship. Today most small churches have just one main service, usually in the morning. If that service is good and strong, then the whole life of the church will be good and strong, but if it is weak and listless, the church life generally will follow suit. If a small church is just going to do one thing to make growth happen, then the one thing to do is to make Sunday worship good.

A good Sunday event will have a major effect on church members, helping to make them positive, alive and joyful; it will do more than anything else to help their faith come alive and deepen their commitment. It will stimulate them into new areas of belief, prayer, spirituality, mission involvement and church life generally.

Good Sunday worship, however, will have more than a congregational effect, it will also have a mission effect. Virtually all churches get a number of visitors, one-off attenders, friends of members, serious seekers, baptism, funeral and wedding contacts, etc, passing through. For the majority of these, no matter what happened in church it would never lead to real interest and conversion, simply because the majority do not want Christ in their lives. At the moment, however, only a minute percentage of these 'passers through' are finding anything to arrest their attention and speak to them. If Sunday worship can be turned into a good event, then a number of these folk will come again and will eventually be converted and added to the small church.

To create good worship does not demand anything elaborate, flashy or way out; it can be very simple, and it is well within the reach of the humblest small urban church. It does however call for sacrifice, a commitment to self-improvement (especially on the part of the minister) and brutal honesty in analysing what is good and what is not good. This change of heart starts off with the observation that clearly what goes on in most small churches is not very good, or else there wouldn't be so many small churches. A good Sunday service can be built around the three 'W's' of Welcome, Worship and Word.

Welcome

Some people cannot stand to be welcomed, having first names pushed at them, or being fussed over. They prefer to slip into quietness, quietly; they like to be anonymous individuals before God. Such people are a small minority, but they are massively catered for in the churches today, especially in the Church of England. We are wonderful at being cold (in more ways than one), distant and hesitant; we are embarrassed by normal, warm humanity. For every person I have discovered who felt threatened by a warm welcome, I have discovered thirty who felt genuinely touched by it. For many of these people their first visit to church in years got off to a really good start with a warm and interested welcome at the door.

This all sounds very simple, but we are very poor at it. Most churches which manage to do it well actually have to delegate people with the right sort of personality, stick them in the right place in the building and warn them to ignore all other demands on their attention and to say 'welcome'. If no one can or will do it, the task is important enough for the minister to do it himself. Most congregations and clergy think of themselves as being very friendly, and they are—to each other. Someone in every church has got to say 'new people are a priority'.

Ideally church wardens should play a key role in this ministry but unfortunately, people who become church officers often develop the habit of constantly discussing internal business matters. Some go even further and become paper clutchers, forever wandering around church entrance lobbies clutching lists, forms, agendas, etc. Church welcomers need to be protected from paper clutchers (to say nothing of the rest of the church).

Coffee served after the service is virtually a must these days. There is no need for lack of plumbing or space (what small church hasn't got lots of spare space taken up with pews used once a year?) to be an insurmountable obstacle. However, one of the worst things that can happen is for new people to be effectively rooted to the spot by a cup of hot coffee with no one talking to them; the whole thing then simply emphasises their embarrassed isolation.

Worship

The general quality of worship is one of the real lows in the life of the church today. It should be one of the highs, as God's people come together to be with him in holiness and joy. In fact many come to it not with expectancy but with a sense of gritting their teeth, and leave with a sensation of relief that their duty is done. Many simply spend the time in a trance of indifference where only thirty per cent of their being is actually alive; having been trained by experience to expect little they go home nicely satisfied; millions have simply stopped coming.

All services will contain something that doesn't interest certain people, and everyone will probably find that certain parts of any service do not appeal to them. It is possible, however, to cut out the huge slices of dullness that haunt much of our worship, and to inject new life. This sort of transfusion does not depend on the availability of music and drama groups, etc, nor on a sudden influx of lively new members. Huge improvements can be made by any church.

The personality of leaders and speakers needs to come through and be alive. Humanity is a vital part of Christian worship, and other people respond warmly to human warmth. The way in which many worship leaders almost screen off their personalities is profoundly misleading. The person leading should move around, have plenty of voice inflexion, he or she should stand or sit fairly close to the congregation (even if it means moving stalls), and (very important) should smile a lot.

The basic form or shape of the service should be fairly simple and straightforward. The shape of Anglican liturgy is excellent but the detail is incredibly wordy and fiddles around far too much. The result is an ASB which reads like a liturgical telephone directory, and feels like a worshipful tombstone. Try to avoid the boring repetition of long wordy slabs, eg the Creed and Eucharistic prayers; these are classic moments of congregation 'nodd-off'.

Music is of fundamental importance. Anything which simply is not working, eg chanting and dusty and unfamiliar hymns, etc, needs to be gradually phased out. There are about 150 to 200 good traditional hymns; the rest do not deserve to be forced on to people who do not know them or enjoy them. Contrary to what we have often been taught, the tune is at least as important as the words. Basically we need to offer people a limited range of good hymns. There is lots of excellent renewal music in both the Catholic and Protestant traditions, and this has massive potential appeal when used carefully. Many congregations actually need to be trained into singing well, singing strongly and joyfully. Good music and singing in any church is dynamite.

At the moment there is a great emphasis on having different musicians. Drums, flutes, violins and electric guitars are almost a status symbol for the successful church. Of course, it's lovely to have people with gifts like these, but it is not essential, which is just as well for the small struggling church. We started out with a damp organ and an ancient piano, but we had people who wanted to sing. I've seen music groups consisting of a piano and half a dozen enthusiastic singers have a much more dynamic effect on a congregation than multi-instrumental ones. The key to a good musical worship life is good singing. If the material is good, manageable and fresh, if the leadership is strong and enthusiastic, and if the congregation are not allowed to get away with sloppiness and apathy, even the smallest and most depleted church can have good music.

Bible reading is another classic 'nod-off' point, so readings need to be short and well done. The impact of Bible reading can be greatly enhanced by the occasional use of background music, by the interplay of two or more voices or by grouping two or three short readings, all following a central theme, in one block.

If a service is to become an event then it needs to have atmosphere and mood. Virtually everyone at some stage finds quiet peacefulness a very helpful backdrop to worship. Such a mood can be encouraged by the use of silence, meditative music (either live or taped) or the use of a helpful visual image such as a single candle in a darkened building. At the other end of the scale brightness and joy are equally vital; large colourful pictures, hand clapping, tambourines and the injection of laughter all have an important part to play. Simple dramas, film strips, taped messages or letters from distant members can all be helpful and there's still a place for smells and bells.

Testimonies, or interviews can be useful. Ordinary people, ie the ones who don't wear dog collars, can have a very warm impact when they get up to speak. Many churches are now regularly encouraging lay people to give interviews or to speak directly, not just about their conversion, but about all sorts of things that God is doing in their lives. Frankly, I have consistently discovered this to be one of the most positive elements in the worship, and the least dramatic or spectacular testimonies are usually the most effective.

Sit the congregation together near the front. At one time the congregation at St Augustine's were scattered like so many rock pools left behind on a huge beach by the retreating tide. I converted the church wardens to the idea of getting people to sit together at the front, then together we worked on the church council. I moved my stall and the communion table closer to them, and after repeated persuasion, hanging up of notices, etc, and a consistent example being set by lay leaders, they moved closer to me. If we had done nothing else to raise the quality of our worship, this one single step would still have created a much-improved worship event. I always mention this when I go to other churches, and virtually everybody agrees with me, but hardly anything is ever done about it.

Word

Archbishop Temple once said that the Church of England was in danger of dying of good taste. This is nowhere truer than in our preaching. All growth, renewal and spiritual rehabilitation depends on enthusiastic and popular style of preaching. Today we frown on enthusiasm and look down on simple Daily-Mirror-type communication. Much of our style, vocabulary, and feel is towards the well-educated *Independent* readers. The art of preaching is one of the most neglected skills in the church. When we recruit people for ministry we don't bother about recruiting preachers and much of the in-service training is at best thin on preaching. The church ministry to the working classes needs good preachers; people full of power, conviction, passion and persuasion.

A preacher has got to be an actor, a salesman, a doctor, a priest, and a good friend all in one. Many have downgraded the whole preaching moment into a brief, subdued little homily, and in so doing have thrown away one of the church-growth gardener's most important tools. Preaching is important enough to demand a good deal of our time and attention. I continually try to work at improving my skills in this area (although members of our congregation might be surprised by this statement). I notice good communicators and try to copy them, I discuss with others the effectiveness, or lack of it, of my own attempts at communication. Long ago I worked out what my biggest failings are (I go on too long, and I often use humour too much and in the wrong places) and I constantly try to work at them. I used to have a grim countenance during much of my preaching; my wife told me to smile more, so week after week I wrote 'SMILE' in big red letters at the top of my notes and eventually it began to work. Frankly, I will try anything if it will gain people's attention, hold their interest and give me an opportunity to communicate the best news in the world, that Jesus loves us.

I will never be an expert preacher and am certainly not in a position to lecture others. However, over the years I have tried to work out a few useful guidelines which I turn to when my preaching gets a bit wayward, and which I try to share with people entering the preaching ministry at St Augustine's. I offer them here to anyone who might find them useful.

The preacher is a larger-than-life figure; he or she has got to reject the temptation to be 'normal' and fade into the background. The use of body, face, hands, voice, etc, has all got to be larger than normal life. This doesn't mean being noisy all the time; it may mean being quieter than normal quiet, or slower than normal slow.

Sermons should have the same 'wallpaper' as the congregation: that is, they should reflect the everyday cultural feel of the listeners. Jesus provides the ultimate example of a simple (but not simplistic) use of ordinary life to illustrate and ground his preaching. His parables were taken from agriculture, the market-place and family life. Ours should be taken from the TV, supermarket, sport and leisure and also from family life.

Visual aids are very valuable. They can be almost anything from blackboard to flip-chart to overhead projector. The best ones are big and colourful. Ordinary objects, actual people and pieces of the building can all make excellent props. These will all make the sermon more enjoyable, clear and memorable.

Two very useful skills that most of us need to practise are the ability to make people laugh, and also the ability to make people stop and be aware.

One of the most daunting tasks facing any of us is preaching for a verdict—exhorting people to make some positive step, be it initial conversion or a further step of deeper commitment along the way. I have made a point of obtaining training for this particular area of preaching and have found it to be invaluable, especially in the rediscovery of the old preaching themes, eg the cross of Christ; the Second Coming; the reality of death; the signs of the times. These were the themes of the Wesleys, the Ranters and the great Revivalists. In our sophistication today we look down on them, yet they have great power, and they are actually of great interest to people.

Preaching in a primarily working-class situation, we try to communicate in as simple and effective a way as possible, while at the same time trying to avoid the sin of patronising or belittling our listeners. The three-step plan that we try to work at is:

Information — Get across the basic message, the one essential piece of information.

Illustration   — Bible stories, parables, anecdotes, jokes, etc, to illustrate the one main point.

Application — Ground the whole thing in real people's real seven-day-week lives.

For preachers and congregation, the sermon need not be something to be got through. Both need to work and pray hard at it, but it can and should be one of the highlights in the life of the church.

There is much more that could be said about worship, such as the use of healing, gifts of the Spirit and the development of such special worship events as bereavement services, pram services, peace vigils and evangelistic guest services. The limited scope of one book, however, does not fully allow for this. There are some excellent books on the market that are given over entirely to this subject, my favourite being *Liturgy and Liberty* by John Leach.[7]

Making changes to any church's worship pattern is one of the most sensitive areas we can enter into. Virtually all churches have a strong worship tradition, and these are not always ancient denominational ones. Many churches today are enslaved to a heavy charismatic worship tradition that is often designed to suit middle-class, middle-aged insiders. This sort of tradition can be just as off-putting to newcomers as can the *Book of Common Prayer*.

If the leadership is clear-sighted, patient and willing to do lots of listening and talking, changes can be introduced. Talk first to God, then to the main lay leaders, then the opinion formers, and finally to the whole congregation and things will happen. I often think back to one very moving incident. As the feel of worship gradually altered at St Augustine's some people were getting increasingly disturbed. I decided it was best out in the open and so called a meeting. The meeting began with the choirmaster, a key person in the church for over thirty years, standing up and saying he had prayed about it and felt the new way was God's way. The meeting closed with silence, with amazement and with prayer.

Establishing a church as family

The average church is a fairly loose collection of religious individuals. They may be used to smiling at each other, and perhaps using a first or second name by way of acknowledgement on a Sunday morning, but for many church attenders that's about as far as it goes. Conversation, where it exists, usually floats on a veneer of superficiality, the result being that people hardly get to know each other at a deep level. The New Testament speaks about the church as a household where everyone belongs, as a flock where each sheep has got its own name, as a building where every individual block has got a vital space to fill. Furthermore, our experience of life tells us all that the truly satisfying experiences of human intercourse are the ones that go on at a deep level. Thus both the Bible and life lead us towards the concept of a church as a family.

In the urban areas where loneliness and rejection are commonplace, where people drift in and out of casual relationships, where the needy often experience the 'caring professions' only in a very formal manner during office hours, and where the majority of people feel shunned by the churches, there is a tremendous need for the church as family.

As with each of the other strategic steps forward, the work needs to begin with the church leader and with his or her family if they have one. The sense of friendliness, acceptance and welcome which characterises all good families needs to begin in the centre with the leadership, and work out.

The early phase

At the centre of our loose collection of religious individuals there will be certain key people. They may form a core group, or several core groups, or they may have the potential to form a core group. If the person who stands at the heart of the group is cold and stand-offish, then the group and thus the church will tend to follow the pattern. If this central person is grim and dour, or 'charismatic intense' and unattractive, then again this will work its way out. However, if a leader who is committed to warmth and love and to being a fairly relaxed normal person, while maintaining a rich spirituality, installs himself/herself at the heart of the core, the core will warm up. It also will start to smile, to invite people round for meals, to call in for a pint after meetings, etc. There is a three-step movement here for the leader to follow:

1. Find out the key people for the future of the church, and install yourself at the heart of them. Make it clear that you want, indeed

need their personal friendship. Spend time with them outside set church activities.

2. Set the tone and the style for this group. Help everyone to feel relaxed. Let friendliness and openness flow out. Share real personal things yourself and ask direct questions to lead them into doing the same thing. Make it clear that it is very much the done thing to talk about God, and to pray together.

3. Lead the group away from exclusiveness and into growth. Force its members to look out and draw others in. Encourage other church members to want to become part of the warm core of the church.

When it comes to turning a church into a family, small urban churches have a huge advantage. The fact that there are fewer people, that they probably have quite a lot of shared memories of church life and family members, etc, is a very real strength, and needs to be fully developed.

The work of turning a church into a family can be gradually developed by:

Stressing the use of first names—if Christians can't use Christian names, then who can?

Getting people to invite each other round for coffee.

Preaching along the theme of being a church family.

Building 'human-meeting' features into Sunday, such as a careful use of the Peace, mentioning birthdays and anniversaries, introducing the personal touch to intercessions, using testimonies and interviews, serving coffee after the service.

A very valuable part of this whole movement is the setting up of church family social events; parties, video-evenings, spring fairs, coach trips, rambles, discos, etc, all have a part to play. Sadly many churches look down on social events, or sometimes the 'spiritual ones' leave it to the others. This negative attitude displays a profound misunderstanding of human nature. God does not live in a religious vacuum, he lives in the everyday laughing and crying, talking and listening, eating and drinking of his people. In our case we initially warmed up, and continued as a noisy hectic family with the social and spiritual proceeding together.

It's not easy getting the balance right between social and spiritual; some of us, sometimes (but not always) the men especially, get too strong on the social and a bit slack on the spiritual. At the other extreme there have been some who have been too dismissive of the social life and wanted to force people into their own religious shape. As with everything else the true and healthy path usually lies down the middle. We have had visitors from 'social life' churches commenting on our strong spiritual life, and others from very 'spiritual' churches admiring our strong social life. Certainly I find it a very salty and powerful picture when I walk into my local working men's club during the season of Lent and see a group of our men sitting around a table full of pints of orange juice and lemonade.

Celebration, congregation and cell

To have a full experience of being a living part of the church we need to experience it at celebration, congregation and cell level. Of these three the congregation is the most familiar. A reasonable number of people, ie forty plus including children, meeting on a fairly regular basis gives a necessary minimum experience of being part of the family. However, we need to broaden this experience in both directions.

Over the last year or so we have started working with two other congregations from working-class areas, to create occasional large-scale Christian events. There are lots of large-scale events around today, Spring Harvest and Greenbelt being of course the biggest and most successful. As well as those two giants, there is a growing practice of bigger churches staging large-scale celebrations. It would have been easy for us to go along to such events, but we decided it would be more meaning-ful for us to work to create something of particular relevance to working-class churches and to invite the big brothers to us for a change. Thus we have organised Christian marches against the Poll Tax, teaching seminars and city-wide worship events. These occasions can give great inspiration to our often beleaguered congregations. People suddenly realise that they are actually part of a huge movement. They enjoy a quality of worship and teaching often beyond their normal resources. They bump into work colleagues and old acquaintances, and suddenly realise that they are members of the family too. In short, they have a par-ticularly powerful experience which cannot supplant the con-gregational bread and butter, but can supplement it.

On the other side of the congregation there is the small group or cell. Virtually all church growth thinkers are united in arguing the importance of small study or fellowship groups. Johan Lukasse's book *Churches with Roots* describes his extensive church planting work in Belgium.[8] It argues in almost every chapter for the importance of groups in evangelism, nurturing of new Chris-tians, training of disciples and maintaining healthy fellowship. Some years ago Eddie Gibbs took an initial sample of 131 churches and came to the conclusion that 'this small sample indicates that starting groups does not in itself guarantee growth, but that if you do have groups then there is a higher probability that you are a growing church.'[9]

Small groups of Christians meeting in homes to pray, sing, read the Bible, share experiences and socialise are ideal for offer-ing the depth and intimacy of fellowship and Christian family life that cannot be found in a congregational gathering. In small groups people have the confidence to talk, ask questions, to express deep feelings. Such groups nurture future leaders; they stimulate loving and caring for each other. Small groups are flexible; they can respond in a spontaneous fashion to one-off situations and individuals. They are the ideal environment for experimenting with gifts and abilities.

Despite what is often said, small groups can flourish in working-class areas, and working-class people can make excellent leaders. A handful of people was already meeting at St Augustine's when we arrived. When we joined it made the group 'safe' for a few others to join. I am amazed when I hear of clergy speaking about Bible study groups meeting in their church but about how they have nothing to do with them. Our group was invaluable to me and to the church as a whole, and my getting involved established it as the key mid-week activity in the life of the church. As members of the congregation began to respond to Sunday worship and teaching, the mid-week fellowship group, which had now moved to the vicarage, became the natural nursery to which to introduce them. When the group had built up into the twenties it was time to divide into two. This first splitting of groups was our most difficult and not very well handled by me as I allowed one group to start out far too small. Since then we have continued to grow to a point where we now have nine house groups plus a mid-week morning Communion service which is in effect like a house group for those who attend. We also have nurture groups, a young people's house group, Mother's Union and Pensioners' groups, all of which supplement the central and key role of our house groups. Not everyone is a small-group person, and we find that men in particular have often got to be persuaded into it. The testimony of our members more than our clergy is that it is the groups that have made the church strong. I would add to this my own personal verdict that the people who are part of groups are more likely to emerge as disciples of Jesus than as just church members.

At least one parish fellowship, Bible study, prayer group or whatever should be established, preferably in a welcoming homely atmosphere. This should be a main priority, taking prominence over other mid-week groups, and getting good preparation time from the leadership. Too many leaders have tried to develop this sort of group and have given up too soon. If the first attempt flops, then stop it; try to discover why it flopped, getting honest answers to questions; take advice from the outside, find two or three others who believe in such a group, and start it again, in a different guise.

When a church becomes a family four big things happen:

The sense of unity and commitment to a common purpose grows.

People in need in the church start to receive much more extensive love, practical help and prayer support.

The whole experience of being a Christian and member of a church becomes more real and enjoyable to church members.

Christianity and the small church in particular becomes more attractive to non-members.

Outside support

If the small urban church receives no outside help at all from the wider church, there is still a great deal that can be done to produce growth, for the greatest source of all outside help is the power of God. If we spent as much time trying to get miracles out of God as we do trying to get money out of the Church Urban Fund, great things would happen.

Praise God, however, that the local small church is not on its own. Outside support is available from different sources, from caring individuals, from other churches, from denominational support structures, from national mission organisations and from charities. The wider church is full of untapped resources of people, energy, time, experience, gifts and money.

Much of the wider church does not want to share its material and spiritual wealth, because it is self-centred instead of God-centred. There are many Christians and churches in suburbia that want to go on with ever bigger buildings, worship events and congregations. This gives them an ever greater sense of accomplishment, pride and superiority, but it has precious little to do with the incarnation-orientated mission of Jesus. However, there is a growing minority of Christians who are willing to give to small mission churches. Their giving will have to be costly if it is to be effective, and it needs to be carefully targeted if it is to be fruitful. There are three particular points in the life of the local church into which resources need to be directed.

Leadership

The leaders of small churches are under terrific pressure. They are often very isolated, they get exhausted, they feel inadequate in the face of the task and second-rate in the face of other people's success. Their health, their mental stability and their spiritual life all suffer, and their family bears the brunt and pays a large part of the price. It is we, the leaders of small struggling churches in difficult areas, who are the biggest single human key to growth. We need to be stroked, encouraged, congratulated, remembered and generally affirmed by our friends, by our congregation, and by those in authority.

We also need good, practical, down-to-earth training. Every diocese or denominational support structure should have people training church leaders in how to lead their church into growth. Frankly this type of training does not exist; we have a huge weakness here right across the churches today.

We need drawing together into small groups of urban clergy, where encouragement, ministry and sharing of good practices can take place. The providing of the right sort of effective training, and the setting up of the truly helpful support structures is the responsibility of those in authority above the local church level.

Congregation

The building up of our congregational life has been greatly helped by outside support coming through various channels. We have received team visits from other churches, for teaching and renewal weekends. This sharing of testimony, gifts and example has had very positive results. Several strongly established Christians from a more professional background have made a particular commitment to come and be part of St Augustine's. These are the sort of people who are not content to be large-church pew-fodder. They want their contribution to God's church to have a real impact.

Over the years we have had a very special link with St Paul's Church in York, where I served my second curacy. It is a very alive, suburban church. The worshippers at St Paul's have shown a deep love for me, for my family and for the whole of our church. They have given joyfully and sacrificially to St Augustine's, sharing in our tears and our laughter.

Buildings and finance

Seven years ago, St Paul's Church in York sent us £1100 to employ a lay worker. That was a lot of money in those days (since then they have given a far larger amount to our building project), and it came like a bolt out of the blue. Nothing like it had ever happened to St Augustine's before. It had two major effects: it cheered me up tremendously, and it helped to turn St Augustine's into a generous, giving church.

A growing number of affluent churches today are establishing links with small urban and rural ones. Some breathe a sigh of relief when the cry goes up, 'These links aren't just about money, they're about prayer.' One can almost feel the liturgical response 'Thank God for that! We can give them our prayers but don't let them ask for our cash.' Thankfully, there is a growing number of exceptions to this: people who realise that prayer without money is cheap prayer, which cheapens God. The small struggling churches need money to improve buildings, employ extra staff, purchase useful equipment and literature, etc.

The work at St Augustine's has been greatly intensified by financial help from different quarters. Our diocese made a huge and to us inspiring commitment to the building of our new church centre, contributing over a quarter of a million pounds. The money was great, but the support given by key diocesan officials was also vital. Greyfriars church in Reading run a very successful church cafe at the heart of a large and affluent church. When they heard about our attempts to set one up in Otley Road, Bradford, they helped to pay the wages of our caterer. Without their help the project would have collapsed within three months.

Prayer and cash offered together is a wonderful combination. It offers help and encouragement to the receiver, and joy and freedom to the giver.

In establishing the right quality and quantity of support the wider church, both at national and denominational and more local diocesan and circuit levels, has got to decide whether it really believes in the two vital concepts that undergird this whole small church strategy. First, that the mainly working-class areas in the cities, on the outer council estates, and deep in the countryside have a special need for the church to be planted in their midst. The Church of England has set a lead in the last few years, by shifting resources to these areas. The churches generally must develop this initiative. The new vibrant churches with their growing numbers and accumulating wealth must put down roots in the whole land and not just in the prosperous areas.

Secondly, that the church needs to adopt a 'growth mission' attitude in place of the 'maintenance' attitude it holds at present. With the decade of evangelism many churches are realising they need to do some evangelism. Missioners or advisers are appointed, a few projects are planned, but this by itself is far from going over to an evangelistic way of living. We need to develop whole strategies, make fundamental decisions at high level and shift resources not just into urban ministry but into urban evangelism in particular. A church which does some evangelism and has a few evangelistic people available is not the same as an evangelistic church.

In his major book on church growth Eddie Gibbs refers to churches having 'remnantitus', fighting on through constant decline like Custer's last stand. At the other extreme he talks about churches living for some sort of fantasy future.

Between the ghosts of the past and the unlikely fantasies of the future there is a middle way. This is the way of carefully planned, gradual and ongoing church growth. This is the way which combines courage and vision, without at the same time eschewing down-to-earth realism.

To follow this way we need to pray the prayer of a person who knows his weakness, but who has placed faith in a great God. We need to follow a good plan, a sound strategy that we believe will bear fruit. We need to make the commitment, along with others, to a sacrificial living out of the cross. We need to place trust in the God whose will and purpose it is to produce growth in the middle of the wilderness.

Summary: The Irrelevant Church and the World

After reading the Bible and studying our history, the relevance or irrelevance of today's church has to be worked out in the theatre of the contemporary world.

1. As we have seen, ours is a first and second class society. To this we should probably add a super luxury coach to one end of the train, and a cattle truck to the other. Ultimately the church has to occupy every corner of society, but does it have to be quite so massively camped out in the first class compartment? If we take the incarnation seriously, then there will be a shift of resources of power and influence and people. Perhaps God is actually wanting you to get up and move, and perhaps he wants you to tell others about it too.

2. The church needs to be transformed from an institution into a movement; a movement which acts, speaks and lives for our whole nation, but especially for the least well-off. Our 'enterprise culture' has seen a virtual end to council house building, a closing down of educational opportunity

(especially in the inner-cities); the taxation burden has been moved off the shoulders of the rich and on to those of the poor; the National Health Service has been whittled away; social and welfare benefits have been slashed; and all this at a time of growing national wealth. This is the hard tough landscape into which the 'movement church' must advance.

However, the people of the inner-cities, the council estates and the deep countryside need more than social and economic provision. They need their full spiritual inheritance too. This is an inheritance of which they have been denied by the culture, class and traditions of the churches. They have a right given them by God's grace. A right to hear and an opportunity to respond to the gospel in a personal and individual way.

3. The church's mission calls for a powerful and penetrating prophetic voice. The prophetic message needs to be on the lips and in the life-styles of national and church leaders, of pastors and ministers, and of individual church members. We must use national and local media, pulpits, church publications, conferences, house-groups and individual conversations, to introduce God's principles to the church and to the world. We must organise, march and campaign for social justice, fair taxation, decent employment, real care for the sick and elderly. The campaign against Sunday trading, the religious anti-abortion lobby and the Christians against the Poll-Tax have all led the way, now there need to be lots of followers.

4. The church is declining. Its decline is most severe in the very places where it is most needed. Today is a time for us to re-discover the faith, the dynamics and the strategies for growth. God's vision is not necessarily for huge 'mega' churches, but it is a vision for growing churches. Growing

numbers, growing quality of lives, growing impact. In theory it is possible for even the smallest, most traditional church or chapel, in the most difficult of areas, to shift from a maintenance to a mission mode. We need to turn theory into reality. A growing church in a deprived area means more people finding the love of God in words and actions.

The call for movement, for prophecy, for growth is not just the concern of those Christians living in deprived areas. It should be the great concern of all of us. It is the concern of the God of movement, compassion and growth. It is the way of relevance and reality. It is the way of the kingdom.

Notes

1. Roy Pointer, *How Do Churches Grow* (MARC Europe: Bromley, 1984).
2. *To a Rebellious House*—Report of the Church of England Partners in Mission Consultation, 1981.
3. ibid.
4. Peter Brierley, *Christian England* (MARC Europe: London, 1991).
5. Chris Edmondson, *Strategies for Rural Evangelism* (Grove Books: Nottingham, 1989).
6. Michael Wooderson, *The Church Down Our Street* (MARC: Eastbourne, 1989).
7. John Leach, *Liturgy and Liberty* (MARC: Eastbourne, 1989).
8. Johan Lukasse, *Churches with Roots* (MARC: Eastbourne, 1990).
9. Eddie Gibbs, *I Believe in Church Growth* (Hodder & Stoughton: London, 1981).

Postscript

So that's it, folks. Well done if you got this far. Well done if you actually paid for your copy, rather than squeezing a freebie out of me. Well done if something actually happened to you as you read it, because something happened to me as I wrote it.

Before anybody says anything, let me first say that *The Irrelevant Church* is not left wing, Socialist or Marxist, neither is it political. I have tried to ensure that it is not unfair or unbalanced. It's not sloppy or sentimental either. Of course there are lots of things wrong with it, there are mistakes, omissions and there's lots of 'me' in it, but in the main it's true.

The Irrelevant Church is much more than the title of this work. The Irrelevant Church is reality. It makes me cry, and I believe it makes God cry too.

INDEX

British Church Growth Association

The British Church Growth Association was formed in September 1981 by a widely representative group of Christians committed to church growth either as researches, teachers, practitioners or consultants. Following the Lausanne Congress on World Evangelisation in 1974, much interest was aroused in Church Growth thinking, which in turn led to the first UK Church Growth Consultation in 1978. Also during the 1970's a number of denominations had taken some church growth thinking and developed it within their own networks. A number of theological colleges and Bible colleges also began to teach church growth theory, particularly in their missiology departments. The Bible Society had begun to develop church growth courses that were being received enthusiastically. Developments in the work of the Evangelical Alliance led to the setting up of a Church Growth Unit and the publication of a *Church Growth Digest*. This unit drew together a number of leaders involved in the church growth field, but it was agreed to widen its impact by the formation of an association which would be even more comprehensive and effective.

Definition

Church Growth investigates the nature, function, structure, health and multiplication of Christian churches as they relate to the effective implementation of Christ's commission to "Go then to all peoples everywhere and make them my disciples" (Mt 28:19). Church Growth seeks to combine the revealed truths of the Bible with related insights from the contemporary social and behavioural sciences. Although not linked to any one school of church growth it owes much to the formational thinking of Dr Donald McGavran.

Aims

The BCGA aims to help encourage the Church in Britain to move into growth in every dimension. The facilities and resources of the BCGA are available to researchers, consultants, teachers, practitioners and those just setting out in church growth thinking. The Association endeavours to offer practical help as well as encouraging and initiating Church Growth thinking and research.

Activities

The following are among its activities:
— Producing a quarterly journal particularly geared to the British scene with practical, biblical and theoretical articles of help to the churches as well as offering a forum for the sharing of views.
— Producing a number of occasional in-depth papers on a variety of topics.
— Co-publishing books on Church Growth.
— Running a specialist Church Growth book service offering discounted books to members and producing a catalogue of recommended church growth reading.
— Operating a reference system for information and personnel.
— Organising biennial residential conferences on particular topics of Church Growth relevant to the church in this country e.g. Church Planting 1983, Conversion 1985, Bridge Building 1987. Various Conferences have also been held in mainline Europe.
— Encouraging, co-ordinating or organising lectures and seminars on particular subjects or with particular speakers which could be of help to the churches.
— Carrying out research in allied fields and building up a research register of work already done or being undertaken in various centres.

— Monitoring church growth at home and overseas.
— Linking in with a European initiative to share insights peculiar to the continent of Europe.
— Encouraging grass-roots involvement through seventeen regional groups.

Government

The Council of the BCGA is made up of 15 elected members and 7 co-opted members who meet 3 times a year. Although members serve in a personal capacity, the Council aims to be representative of geographical region, denomination and churchmanship, practitioner, researcher and teacher.

The day-to-day running of the Association is carried out by an officer with some secretarial assistance and the active support of members of the Council. The offices are situated at 3a Newnham Street, Bedford MK40 2JR and the telephone number is 0234 327905. The BCGA is a registered charity, no. 28557.

Membership

Membership of the BCGA is open to both individuals and organisations interested in or involoved in the theory or practice of Church Growth. On payment of an annual subscription members are entitled to receive the *Church Growth Digest* (the journal of the Association) four times a year, information about activities through the Newsletters, special discounts on conferences and books, membership of the Church Growth Book Service, voting rights to elect members to the Council every two years, links with other researchers, teachers, practitioners, and consultants on a regional or national level as well as help or advice on allied matters.

The current subscription is £12.50 for individual membership and £25 for organisations or churches.

Further information about the Association and membership is available from the Secretary, British Church Growth Association, 3a Newnham Street, Bedford MK40 2JR.

Restoring The Vision

Edited by Melvin Tinker

Confused and nervous?

Has evangelicalism in the Anglican Church become so broad that it has lost focus? Have yesterday's crusaders become today's conformers? Anglican evangelicals seem confused and nervous, unwilling to hold fast to their convictions in a period in which they are paradoxically gaining the ascendancy. How can evangelicals restore the vision?

This collection of essays pinpoints some of the issues central to Anglican evangelicals. Biblical interpretation; inter-faith dialogue; social ethics; the role of women; ecumenism; these and many other topics are tackled in this readable and competent analysis. What do evangelicals believe about the nature of the Church? The purpose of the ordained ministry? The significance of holy communion?

'True evangelicalism', argues Melvin Tinker, 'lies at the historical, doctrinal and spiritual heart of our national church. It is a position for which evangelicals must be willing to contend.'

Prior to his current position as Anglican Chaplain at Keele University, the *Rev Melvin Tinker* read theology at Oxford, trained for ordination at Wycliffe Hall and served a curacy in Wetherby, Yorkshire. He is a member of the Church of England Evangelical Council.

MARC
Monarch Publications

Your Spiritual Gifts Can Help Your Church Grow

by C Peter Wagner

Discover the spiritual gifts God intends you to exercise within the Body of Christ.

'This is essentially a book on church health', explains Peter Wagner. 'Churches grow because they are healthy. Therefore, developing the dynamic of spiritual gifts in a church – because it is biblical and because it will help make Christians more Christlike, and because it will enhance the health of the Body – should also help churches to grow.'

Spiritual gifts promote wholeness, claims Dr Wagner. He examines each gift in detail and shows how the gifts can become operative in your church now.

Dr C Peter Wagner is Professor of Church Growth at Fuller Theological Seminary School of World Mission. He served as a missionary to Bolivia for 16 years, and has written and edited more than twenty-four books.

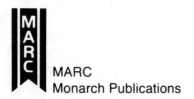

MARC
Monarch Publications

Dynamic Leadership

by Paul Beasley-Murray

Without a vision the people perish.

A church with vision is one that grows. To gain a vision a church needs effective leadership. This book, by one of Britian's most eminent Christians, shows us clearly and biblically how to develop dynamic leaders.

Using many models from the wider world, but, above all, the model of Jesus himself, Paul Beasley-Murray shows us how to lead, and, just as important, who can lead. For truly dynamic leadership is shared in a team, where tasks can be defined, goals accomplished, and the whole church served in a Christ-like way.

This book is profoundly practical. How do you inspire the youth group? Lead a church meeting? Motivate the church for evangelism? Train new believers? Instil Christian values in your community? Here again dynamic leadership is the name of the game.

Reading this book could change your church for ever.

'Excellent...full of practical insights for busy church leaders.'

—**Stephen Gaukroger, author of** *It Makes Sense*

MARC
Monarch Publications